Holiday Money

"Once you've read about TravelMoney you'll wish you were a Nationwide saver."

If you have a Nationwide savings account, there's a unique service that can help you make a quick and easy holiday getaway.

It's called TravelMoney. It means that when you've built up your holiday savings in one of our schemes, you can convert however much money you'd like directly into Thomas Cook travellers cheques and foreign currency. So your savings stay in your account right up to the last minute. All we ask is that you give us 2 to 3 days notice, and we'll do the rest. We call it putting the simplicity back into holidays.

Putting the building back into society.

TRAVEL MONEY

Nationwide

Nationwide Building Society,
New Oxford House, High Holborn,
London WC1V 6PW.

Holiday Money

Wendy Elkington

Published by Rosters Ltd
First Edition 1986

Acknowledgements
The cartoons are reproduced from
FUNNY MONEY by ALAN RALPH
published by Rosters Ltd (1985)

Designed and published by Rosters Ltd
Set by JH Graphics Ltd, Reading
Printed and bound in Great Britain
by Cox & Wyman Ltd, Reading

ISBN 0 9480 3225 1

CONTENTS

INTRODUCTION

"And furthermore under this government the pound in your pocket this year weighs twice as much as it did last year"

Holidays are a major part of most families' budget. Now that it's cheaper to enjoy a fortnight sunning yourself in Spain rather than moaning about the weather at an English seaside resort, more and more Britons are flocking to that great unknown across the water called 'overseas'.

The costs of a foreign holiday have been rising steadily over the years. The big tour operators reckon a two week package holiday for a family of four can slice around £1,500 off your savings. What's more most packages usually include only one meal and no drinks. So unless you are an anorexic camel it's pretty hard not to shell out an extra £250 to £350 in spending money.

Working out the best way to finance your holiday and arrange for an ample supply of foreign currency can be complex. It pays to take a little time doing your homework as the savings you can achieve are quite substantial. Clever financial footwork can make the difference between a holiday on a shoestring and a vacation to remember.

How Much to Take

To give you a rough idea of how much goods and services are likely to cost abroad compared to Britain, have a look at the 'Cost of Holiday Living Chart' produced by travel agents, Thomas Cook. Of course, prices will vary but the figures quoted are an average cost calculated on the basis of charges collated by Thomas Cook representatives throughout Europe.

The figures should be treated with a pinch of judicious analysis. On the face of it Yugoslavia appears to be the most expensive country. However, if you dig more closely into the statistics you'll discover this is only because car hire is so dear – twice as costly as any other European country. Providing you are not planning to hire a car in Yugoslavia, you can enjoy one of the cheapest package holidays in Europe within its borders.

Spain, which as you can see is also excellent value for British visitors, is still the most popular choice for UK citizens. So much so that the Costa Brava could be renamed the Costa Fish'n Chips. Still, Spain's lead is being whittled away by Greece, Italy, Portugal and Yugoslavia which are attracting a growing number of British sun seekers.

Although the Thomas Cook Holiday Living Index is an excellent yardstick, do try to work out your own individual requirements. You may be able to save on petrol and car hire, but need to spend more on food, drink and entertainment. Always try to leave yourself a cushion for unexpected emergencies such as airport tax, customs, as well as more enjoyable spending sprees on presents for you and your friends.

Breadth of Choice

In the good old days when travel was restricted to the wealthy landed gentry, a pouch jangling with gold coins was the best international currency. Now the era of plastic and automation has taken over from the bygone days of heavy metal and paper money.

Today's traveller can choose from a vast array of plastic cards, cheques and currencies. Each has its pros and cons. Try to work out the best mix to suit your requirements and the facilities available in the resort. Holiday Money will guide your through the foreign currency maze and help you stretch those hard earned pounds to their full value.

Cost of Holiday Living Index — Summer 1985

Information compiled & presented by Thomas Cook

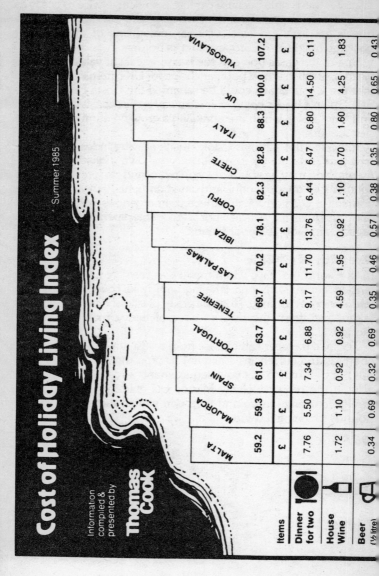

Items	MALTA	MAJORCA	SPAIN	PORTUGAL	TENERIFE	LAS PALMAS	IBIZA	CORFU	CRETE	ITALY	UK	YUGOSLAVIA
	59.2	59.3	61.8	63.7	69.7	70.2	78.1	82.3	82.8	88.3	100.0	107.2
	3	3	3	3	3	3	3	3	3	3	3	3
Dinner for two	7.76	5.50	7.34	6.88	9.17	11.70	13.76	6.44	6.47	6.80	14.50	6.11
House Wine	1.72	1.10	0.92	0.92	4.59	1.95	0.92	1.10	0.70	1.60	4.25	1.83
Beer (½ litre)	0.34	0.69	0.32	0.69	0.35	0.46	0.57	0.38	0.35	0.80	0.65	0.43

10

Soft Drink	0.43	0.28	0.37	0.37	0.32	0.34	0.34	0.35	0.24	0.48	0.45	0.31
Coffee	0.43	0.28	0.32	0.23	0.32	0.23	0.32	0.29	0.24	0.32	0.60	0.24
Tea	0.34	0.28	0.32	0.32	0.28	0.23	0.32	0.29	0.24	0.28	0.40	0.24
Camera Film	2.88	3.30	2.29	3.67	2.45	3.44	3.30	3.82	2.94	2.36	2.51	2.57
Sun Cream	2.84	2.82	2.57	2.75	2.87	2.93	2.78	2.35	2.47	2.18	3.59	1.31
5 Postcards	0.86	1.03	0.92	1.03	1.05	1.03	0.92	0.88	0.95	0.88	1.35	1.22
Car Hire (Per Week)	66.38	81.88	86.38	83.49	72.94	72.94	81.88	159.76	159.76	148.12	108.50	225.00
Petrol (20 litres)	8.72	8.53	9.17	10.00	6.97	6.88	8.72	6.68	7.76	10.40	8.97	7.22
WEIGHTED TOTAL FOR ONE WEEK	174.36	174.84	182.25	187.74	205.28	206.85	230.04	242.38	243.95	260.26	294.67	316.00

Thomas Cook's Cost of Holiday Living Index is based on dinner for two (plus one bottle of wine) each night; 2 cups of coffee and tea, 4 beers and 2 soft drinks each day for a week; 1 roll of 24 print camera film, 1 bottle of suncream, 5 postcards (including postage); car hire for a week and 20 litres of petrol.

A week's total is given and shown in the graph against an index of cost for a typical holiday resort in the UK. Exchange rates are those current on May 30 1985.

Source: Thomas Cook Financial Services Division

"My diagnosis MR PRENDERGAST is excessive WITHDRAWAL SYMPTOMS ..."

Choosing a summer holiday is almost as much fun as actually going away. Leafing through the catalogues you can give your imagination free rein – forgetting about the constraints of your pocket book. Do take care, you don't want to still be paying for your summer holiday the following Christmas.

Counting the Cost

A package holiday abroad for a family of four will set you back at least £1,000. That's before taking into account spending money. Families staying in hotels can expect an extra bill of £250 to £350, while those taking a self-catering package may need up to £500. So, the average family is looking at a total of around £1,500. While top wage earners might be able to pay this amount out of one month's salary, for most of us it's a question of spreading the cost over a much longer period.

Saving Schemes

The best bet is to save. There are plenty of plans to choose from. Most high-street banks pay regular savers a bonus rate of interest. Normally to qualify you need to save the same amount each month, although some schemes are more flexible allowing you to miss the odd payment without penalty. Usually the minimum is £10 a month and you can expect to earn a premium rate of interest of 1% to 2% above the normal deposit rate. Check to see if there are any restrictions on withdrawing cash. Some plans insist on a month's notice. So make sure you co-ordinate the notice period with the holiday payment date.

As an alternative try your favourite building society. Most run regular savings schemes or offer what are called 'subscription shares'. But the plans vary a lot. Check whether you can miss the occasional payment and also whether you can vary the amount paid in. Also, scrutinise the withdrawal rules. The extra interest carrot is often balanced by the stick of only being allowed access to your money once a year or having to give a month's notice.

Often the easiest option is to open a straight forward instant access high interest account. You may earn a little less interest, but not enough to make any appreciable difference and the added flexibility is worth its weight in gold.

Borrowing from the Bank

If you realise from the start you won't be able to save enough to cover the full holiday cost, then look at a special account offered by most banks which pays interest on your savings and lets you have an automatic loan when you need to. These accounts have various names, for example Barclays' Cashplan, Lloyds' Cash-flow and Midland's Save and Borrow. Usually you receive a higher rate than on the normal deposits and borrowing charges in line with bank credit cards.

You have to agree to save a set amount each month. In return, you can borrow money automatically without having to ask for a loan. Some banks restrict the amount you can borrow to, say, 30 times your monthly payment. That means if you save £30 a month, you'll be able to borrow up to £900. The maximum loan limit varies. The ceiling is in the region of £5,000, so you couldn't finance round-the-world trips for a family of four.

Building Societies

Building societies are to be allowed much greater freedom in 1987. Meanwhile many have linked up with finance houses to package loan schemes. You usually pay less than if you went direct to the finance house. Make sure you ask what the true rate (or annual percentage rate of credit) is before signing on the dotted line. It can be more expensive than using your credit card.

Credit Card

Providing your credit limit can stand it, paying for your holiday by

Access, Barclaycard or Trustcard makes good sense. You've the added protection under the Consumer Credit Act that if the tour operator goes bust, the credit card company will give you a refund. While the interest rate for a one year loan is on the high side, if you pay off the holiday in less than 12 months, the true cost is comparatively reasonable.

Overdrafts

If you can persuade your bank manager to let you overdraw your account to pay for your holiday, this can be a cheap payment method. But there are drawbacks. first, some banks have increased their charges to between 5% and 7% over base rate, compared with between 3% and 7% in the past. Also, once your account is overdrawn, you have to pay bank charges and these can mount up very quickly. You will probably have to pay an arrangement fee of around £10 to £20 as well. So although the interest rate on overdrafts may be the cheapest, the extra charges can make it quite expensive.

Personal Loans

If you ask your bank manager how to finance your holiday then he's likely to suggest a personal loan. This is an expensive and inflexible option. The interest rate is set at the outset and you are locked in. You don't benefit from any subsequent fall. Also, repayments are spread over a set period with regular monthly payments.

Finance Houses

Some secondary banks and finance houses offer loans which can be used to pay for holidays. Their rates are usually among the highest going, often 30% plus, and they are usually fixed throughout the loan term. If you can't find an alternative, you probably can't afford the holiday.

Thomas Cook Travel Card

Thomas Cook has its own credit card. This can be used to pay for any travel or holiday arrangements, travellers cheques, and foreign currency bought at any of 250 shops and bureaux de change.

It works on much the same lines as Barclaycard and Access. The minimum transaction, though, is £50. You have to pay either £10 or 10% of the amount outstanding each month. The credit limit is normally £1,000, although you may get more if your financial standing warrants it. Check the interest rate charged on amounts outstanding. Compare it with that of Barclaycard and Access.

Special Schemes

The innovative Yorshire-based Skipton Building Society launched a special holiday club last year. This gives discounts to its investors. To be eligible for membership, savers must open a Sovereign Shareholders Account, which has a £500 minimum investment but allows instant withdrawals with no penalties. The interest rate paid on savings is not guaranteed, but since launch there has always been a premium of at least 2% over the ordinary deposit rate.

When the Holiday Club was launched it offered a 10% discount to members off all Sovereign Holidays. Then Skipton negotiated a special deal with P&O cruises under which club members booking a P&O holiday are given up to £250, depending on how much they spend. Skipton hopes to add discounts on Rank Holidays which include OSL, Butlins, Wings, and Far Away Holidays and a 10% discount package at Townsend Thoresen's La Manga Club in Spain. La Manga is a highly rated holiday and sports complex just north of the Costa Del Sol, but within easy reach of Malaga airport.

Alliance and Leicester

The newly merged Alliance & Leicester Building Society launched a new package of special offers and discounts in January for all holders of the Alliance & Leicestercard. To qualify for a card you need just £100 in their account. 1986's discounts include £5 free spending money for every £100 spent on a Page & Moy holiday, up to £20 discount on Ladbroke Group's holidays and commission free Thomas Cook travellers cheques.

17

Visa Travel Vouchers

A new development is travel vouchers issued by VISA banks and available from travel agents. They can be used to prepay a range of travel services and holiday basics. The system is simple, you prepay your hotel bill. In return your travel agent will give you a voucher made out in the hotel's local currency. When you get to the hotel you simply hand over your voucher.

As far as the hotel is concerned it is similar to receiving a cheque drawn against the issuing VISA bank. The hotel will bank the voucher and money will be transferred into its account in settlement.

There is a replacement service available round the clock if your vouchers are lost or stolen. The drawback is that you are paying for services in advance without gaining any discount for prepayment. You are also locked into the rate of exchange ruling when you bought the voucher, but that can work either in your credit or to your disadvantage depending on developments on international currency markets.

Chapter 2

UNDER COVER

"Will the insurance on your romantic ski-ing
holidays cover a broken heart?"

The major tour operators offer a package insurance policy, details of which can be found in the brochure. The table shows what this costs and what you get for your money.

Package Deals

Tour Operator	Cost per person*	Maximum health cover	Baggage	Money
Thompson	£10.80	£5,00,000	£1000	£200
Intasun	£13.60	unlimited	£1000	£250
Horizon	£12.60	£100,000	£1000	£250
British Airways (Sovereign & Enterprise	£11.45	£1,000,000	£1000	£500
Rank Travel (OSL, Wings)	£11.50	unlimited	£1000	£500
Cosmos Air Holidays	£11.40	unlimited	£1000	£200
Thomas Cook	£12.50	unlimited	£1000	£200

*two week holiday

Policy Checklist

If you book your holiday through a travel agent, he or she may suggest you choose a policy they have arranged. Travel agents earn extra commission from insurance companies for selling travel policies, so work out the sums for yourself.

The main points to check are:

★ Medical Insurance: This is critical. The cost of medical treatment abroad can be far higher than in this country. Some policies now give unlimited cover, others specify a limit. You should look for at least £100,000 worth of cover in Europe and £500,000 if you are going to America.

★ Flight delays. Payment after a 12 hour delay of between £12 and £20.

★ Baggage. £1,000 worth of cover, with a limit of £200 per item. Ample for most occasions, but may need topping up if you have expensive taste in clothes, jewellery or cameras.

★ Non-arrival of baggage. Willingness to pay immediate expenses incurred if airline fails to deliver your luggage on time.

★ Money. Cover for losses of £200 to £500.

★ Cancellation. Read small print as this is the most frequent cause of a claim.

★ Failure of tour operator. Check you are covered and how much. Only included in independent policy.

★ Bankruptcy of airline. Again only included in independent policy. Check cover and sum.

★ Your cancellation rights. Can you cancel without financial penalty and if so under what conditions.

★ Size of the excess. Most policies require the traveller to pay the first part of any claim, typically up to £20.

★ Before you take the policy, check the exclusions.Most companies will exclude cover for pre-existing illnesses, so if you have any recurring illnesses, make sure you tell the company when you take out the policy.

★ Some companies exclude illness or injury due to drink, drugs, pregnancy and attempted suicide. So read the policy carefully.

★ You must report any illness immediately and this applies before you go on holiday as well as while you are away. So if you are ill before you go but are not sure whether you will be able to go away, play safe and tell the company about your illness.

★ Lost money not reported to the police within 24 hours is often excluded – if the local police won't give you a written note to confirm you have spoken to them, ask your resort rep or hotel management.

★ Air ambulance service. Useful if you fall seriously ill and need to come back to Britain for treatment.

There are certain advantages in taking the cover offered by the tour operator. If you do run into a problem, the resort representative will have a better chance of sorting it out quickly through head office than you will have battling alone. Also, the tour operators have considerable muscle with insurance companies whose policy they sell. This can mean a quicker service if you need to claim. Some tour operators try to cut corners to keep prices down and one area they prune is insurance cover. So do a little homework before signing on the dotted line.

Do-It-Yourself Options

If you are going solo then buy your insurance from a broker or your bank. There's plenty of choice. The table below shows what some of the big insurance companies and high-street banks offer:

Company	Cost % £	Maximum Health Cover £	Baggage £	Money £
Barclays	13.20	500,000	1,000	200
General Accident	15.00	100,000	2,000	500
Lloyds	13.95	1,000,000	1,000	250
Nat West	11.45	1,000,000	1,000	250
Norwich Union	17.00	500,000	1,500	300
Midland	13.40	500,000	1,250	300
Prudential	18.00	250,000	1,000	250

Handy Hints

1. Buy your holiday through an ABTA (Association of British Travel Agents) member. They have a bond scheme to pay out in case of default.
2. Book through a large well-known company such as Thomas Cook, American Express, Hogg Robinson, Pickfords or A.T. Mays. They provide schemes which either give you your money back or an alternative holiday if your package operator goes bust.
3. Pay for part of the holiday, at least £100 with your credit card. If the tour operator goes bust, the credit card company will pay up. Barclaycard holders enjoy special cover and will be compensated if the operator goes bust before they have had their holiday.
4. Tailored insurance packages. American Express provides a useful alternative to shopping around for regular travellers. For a single premium of £45 you enjoy medical cover of up to £1m for all the family when you travel together. Plus a range of useful features. Called the Centurion Assistance package it includes emergency repatriation, family care and emergency personal assistance. For an extra £25 you can buy personal travel insurance and another £35 will get you emergency vehicle assistance.
5. Credit card cover. It can be a nightmare trying to contact several credit card companies from your holiday resort if your

cards are lost or stolen. A number of schemes are on the market. Access launched Cardwise in 1985 for its own cardholders. For £6 a year you can register all your bits of plastic and one telephone call to Access HQ in Southend will result in all the issuers being informed of your loss. Diners club run a similar scheme for £6 a year or £16 for three years.

Your Car Abroad

1. Extend your existing comprehensive cover by asking the insurance company for a so-called green card. Cost ranges from £10 to £20 depending on your travel plans.
2. If you are visiting Spain, get a bail bond just to be on the safe side. You'll pay a few pounds for up to £2,000 worth of cover but it will prevent your holiday being ruined by a sojourn in a Spanish jail.
3. Buy some emergency assistance cover. Best known schemes are: AA's Five Star, RAC Travellers Bond, Europ Assistance, GESA Assistance and Mondial Assistance. You can expect to pay around £60 to £100 to cover a family of four and the car over a fortnight.

A good policy will give you cover for the following:

- Hotel accommodation while repairs are underway
- Journey continuation/get you home cost
- Vehicle repatriation
- Roadside assistance
- Temporary replacement vehicle
- Spare parts delivery
- Provide an air ambulance service to fly a badly injured person back to the UK.

"GIMME a fistful of DOLLARS"

You can bet your last pound coin that when you arrive at your destination you'll need some local money. There's always the outstretched porter's hand or the bleeping call box as you try to sort out your hotel reservation. Many packaged holidays start on Saturday. You arrive after lunch, only to find you can't get inside a banking hall until Monday morning. So you end up, cashing a travellers cheque at the hotel reception where you'll be given an abysmal rate of exchange and pay hefty commission charges.

Counting the Cost

So even if you have chosen the packaged holiday route take some spare foreign currency, preferably in small denominations. There are several places to buy foreign currency. You can choose from your own high street bank, a bureau de change, the post office, selected building societies, foreign banks branches in this country, American Express offices and Thomas Cook branches. As you can see from the table the total costs involved vary considerably.

A good tip to remember is that some building societies have begun to sell foreign currency and being mutual organisations they can provide their customers with an exceptionally good deal. The Scarborough Building Society, for example, sells foreign currency of any amount for a fee of £1. Other societies which have nipped on the foreign currency bandwagon include Nationwide, West of England, Midshire, Heart of England, Peterborough and Furness.

Organisation	Cost of Changing £100	Cost of Changing £1,000	Minimum Charge	Commission	Extra Charges
American Express	£1	£1	£1 max.	—	Fee normally waived for orders under £10
Barclays	75p	£5	75p	½%	Maximum charge £10
Lloyds	£1	£5	£1	½%	
Midland	£2	£15	£1	2%	Maximum charge £15
Nat West	£1.25	£1.25	£1.25	—	£3 extra for urgent orders
Royal Bank of Scotland	£1	£5	50p*	—	£1 charge on orders worth between £10 and £500
Thomas Cook	£1	£10	£1	1%	
Trustee Savings Bank	£1	£5	£1	½%	Maximum charge £10

* for up to £10 worth of currency.

Finally, try to allow at least a week for your currency to arrive. Although most banks will probably be able to supply dollars and pesetas on demand, many smaller branches will have to wait for their order to be sent from a regional centre. More exotic currencies, such as yen or Saudi riyals may take a fortnight to wing their way round the country to your local branch.

Exchange Rates

Rates of exchange leap around like scalded cats. For example, the dollar slumped 20% against the pound in the first nine months of 1985. Gyrations of this proportion can cause quite a headache. They throw out of synch the tour operators costs and may land you with a bill for surcharges.

On the whole personal customers get a pretty raw deal compared to large corporations when they buy foreign currency. They are charged a wide spread between the price at which the bank will sell them currency and the sum at which they are prepared to buy it back. This spread varies between 2% and 3%. Don't be mislead by the rates of exchange published in newspapers, these only apply to commercial transactions. Look instead for a board listing the tourist rates.

You'll find the best rate of exchange if you go to a branch of a foreign bank from the country you plan to visit. Some also waive their commission charges. Most of the world's major banks have branches either in the City of London or the West End. Below are a list of addresses of foreign bank branches for the most popular tourist spots where you can usually buy the local currency more cheaply than at a British high street bank:

Spain
Banco de Bilbao
3 Sloane Street, London SW1
40 King Street, London WC2

Banco Hispano Americano
15 Austin Friars, London EC2

Italy
Banco di Roma
14 Eastcheap, London EC3

France
Credit Lyonnais
84 Queen Victoria Street, London EC4
18 Regent Street, London SW1

Banque National de Paris
8 King William Street, London EC4
60 Brompton Road, London SW3

Portugal
Banco Espirito Santo and Commercial de Lisboa
6th Floor, 4 Fenchurch Street, London EC3

The high street banks offer middle of the road exchange rates. The worst rates are normally given by independent bureau de change. They are open long hours and have high staff costs to cover. Also try to avoid bank branches at airports and ports. These too suffer from high overheads and the additional expenses involved in providing a round-the-clock service.

Currency Restrictions

Some countries restrict the amount of currency tourists bring in, while others have strict rules about how much of their cash you can export. Don't play fast and loose with these regulations. If the customs men find you have more than the allowed sum they may confiscate it and fine you. The table below will keep you on the right side of the law.

Country	Currency	Amount you can take in	Amount you can take out
Australia	Australian Dollar	unlimited	5,000
Austria	Schilling	unlimited	15,000
Belgium	Belgian Franc	unlimited	unlimited
Canada	Canadian Dollar	unlimited	unlimited
Cyprus	Cyprus Pound	50	50
Denmark	Krone	unlimited	5,000
Egypt	Egyptian Pound	20	20
France	French Franc	unlimited	5,000
Germany (West)	Deutschmark	unlimited	unlimited
Greece	Drachma	3,000*	3,000*
India	Rupee	prohibited	prohibited
Ireland	Punt	unlimited	unlimited
Italy	Lira	400,000	400,000
Luxembourg	Luxembourg Franc	unlimited	unlimited
Malta	Maltese Pound	50	25
Morocco	Dirham	prohibited	prohibited

Country	Currency	Amount you can take in	Amount you can take out
Netherlands	Guilder	unlimited	unlimited
Norway	Krone	unlimited	5,000
Portugal	Escudos	5,000	5,000
Russia	Ruble	prohibited	prohibited
Spain	Peseta	unlimited	100,000
Sweden	Krona	Notes of 10,000 prohibited in and out Notes of 1,000 unlimited in and 6,000 out	
Switzerland	Swiss Franc	unlimited	unlimited
Tunisia	Dinar	prohibited	prohibited
Turkey	Lira	unlimited	equivalent of US $1000
USA	Dollar	unlimited	unlimited
Yugoslavia	Dinar	2,500	2,500

*can only take in and out notes of 500 Drachma or under

Source: Barclays Bank

In some communist countries, you may be approached with an offer to buy your sterling at a particularly attractive rate of exchange. This is an offer you can definitely afford to refuse – a night on the tiles in Lubyanka is not to be recommended.

On arrival at some places, particularly the Iron Curtain states, you may be asked to convert a minimum amount of foreign currency into local money when you cross the border. Remember too that you are not allowed to leave the country with any local currency, so make sure you work out exactly how much you need and don't be tempted to cash more. If you do have any unused currency left over at the end of your stay, you will probably have to convert it back to sterling at the airport or border at a very poor rate of exchange.

Taking Sterling Abroad

It's always a good idea to take some sterling with you when you go abroad. If there are any delays when you get back to this country, you may need some extra cash. It will act as a reserve if you overspend when you are on holiday.

Drawbacks of Foreign Cash

The most obvious drawback is security. If your foreign currency is lost or stolen, the best you can hope for is that the loss will be covered by your holiday insurance policy and you'll be refunded on your return home. Most holiday insurance policies cover losses of this sort, although they may make you foot the first £15 and normally limit the cover to £250.

If disaster – or a pickpocket – does strike make sure you report the loss to the police within twenty-four hours. Ask for proof in writing that you made the complaint as you'll need this when you claim for the cash back home. In some countries the police will not provide you with a completed loss form, in which case ask the hotel management or your tour operator to do the honours. A word of warning. Most insurance companies take a hard line on holiday-makers claiming to have lost cash. Inserted in the small print of most policies is the caveat that you must take reasonable care to avoid loss. If you leave your handbag on the beach, go for a swim and find your wallet missing when you come back, the insurance company won't settle your claim.

So it's wise to take precautions – don't carry much money around on the beach or swimming pool, keep your handbag near you in bars, restaurants and discos. British men have never taken to the idea of handbags – but how about money belts – ordinary looking belts with concealed pockets in which to hide notes and coins. These can be an excellent 'safe' for money – the only drawback is that you have to unbelt everything when you want to produce some money.

Cash Shortfall

Banking is an international business, so if you do run short of cash you should be able to arrange for your own bank back home to cable you some extra funds. Before you go abroad ask your bank

Cash Shortfall

Banking is an international business, so if you do run short of cash you should be able to arrange for your own bank back home to cable you some extra funds. Before you go abroad ask your bank manager whether there are reciprocal arrangements with any banks in the country you plan to visit and if so, make a note of the appropriate bank branches in the cities you are visiting.

If you do run out of money and need to contact your own branch, be prepared to pay for this facility. You'll probably have to pay for the cable plus a fixed commission. You should also remember to take along plenty of proof of your identity and domestic bank account. Passport, your English chequebook and cheque guarantee card should do the trick.

Sterling Policies

Provided you have a cheque guarantee card you can walk into any branch of your bank and cash a cheque for £50 per day. If you have a cash dispenser card you can get access to up to £100 a day by simply tapping in your secret personal identification number. Big spenders who need extra cash, can ask the branch to phone their local manager, who will let them know whether you are good for the size of the cheque you have written. You'll end up being charged from £2 to £5 for this facility. You can save this fee by setting up an arrangement in advance.

Chapter 4

TRAVELLERS' CHEQUE POINT

"The bank next door says you've got all the money ..."

Travellers cheques are the most popular way of taking money abroad. The secret of their success is simplicity. You sign the cheques when you buy them in one space where it says 'holder to sign'. Then, when you want to cash one or use it to pay for goods or services, you countersign in the second space where it says 'counter-signature in presence of paying agent'. The wording may vary on each cheque but the meaning will always be the same and sums up the two basic golden rules:

1. Always sign the cheques when you buy them

2. Never countersign them until you want to cash one. Then make sure you sign them in front of the cashier or shop assistant.

Where to Buy Them

Type	Source
American Express	From their own offices, Lloyds Bank branches, Royal Bank of Scotland, NatWest (US$ only), many building societies including Abbey National, Anglia, Britannia, Leeds Permanent and Woolwich.
Visa	Branches of Barclays, Standard Chartered Bank, Bank of Scotland, Trustee Savings Bank, AA offices and some building societies.

Thomas Cook	Branches of Midland, Clydesdale, Northern Bank, some building societies including Nationwide and Alliance & Leicester, Post Offices, Thomas Cook Travel shops.
NatWest	Supplies its own brand of sterling travellers cheques at its own branches. Also in around 700 travel agents and a dozen building societies plus branches of Coutts and Ulster Bank.
Citicorp	Citibank Savings, Co-op Bank, NatWest, ABTA travel agents and some building societies.

Notes

1. On Visa cheques: the name of the issuing bank can be printed on each cheque – Barclays Visa, for example, but all have the familiar blue white and gold Visa symbol.

2. Thomas Cook travellers cheques are endorsed by Mastercard, and Euro Travellers Cheque organisations whose symbols appear on cheques.

Sterling Cheques

These are usually readily available and do not need to be ordered in advance. They usually come in denominations of £10, £20, £50, £100 and occasionally £200. This spread of values should give you enough flexibility to control your spending when abroad. However, American Express and VISA have started supplying their travellers cheques in pre-packs. For example, you may have to buy a pack of five £5 cheques. This can make it more difficult to choose the exact mix of denominations you require. In countries, such as Norway or Malta where commission is charged on each individual cheque cashed, this can be costly.

Foreign Currency Travellers Cheques

Although it is possible to buy cheques in over 20 currencies, some are issued by banks, whose names are not well known outside their own country. It is wise to stick with the better known issuers

Commission free
Travellers Cheques

At the Alliance & Leicester Building
Society you don't have to pay commission
on Thomas Cook Travellers Cheques
if you have an instant access account.
That's a bright idea.

ALLIANCE LEICESTER
A brighter idea altogether.

such as American Express, Thomas Cook, Visa, National West-minster Bank and Citicorp, and remember to order about a week in advance. This gives you plenty of choice as the table shows.

What They Cost to Buy

Most suppliers of travellers cheques charge a flat fee of 1% with a minimum charge of £1 or £2. However, there are variations in commissions and fees. Also, a few places issue travellers cheques free of commission.

Foreign currency travellers cheques generally cost a little more than the sterling variety. National Westminster and Thomas Cook charge 1¼%, American Express add on an extra 50p per trans-action while Lloyds is the most expensive with an extra £2 charge per order.

Best Buy

One of the best buys is to purchase your travellers cheques from one of the limited number of building societies which offer com-mission free cheques to their own customers. It's even worth specially opening an account.

At present the following societies give this perk to savers: Birmingham & Bridgewater, Bristol & West, Chatham, Reliance, Coventry, Leamington Spa, Leeds Permanent, Alliance & Leicester, Scarborough and Sussex Mutual.

You will normally have to pay a second commission when you cash your sterling travellers cheques abroad. There is no commis-sion charge for cashing American Express or Thomas Cook cheques at their own overseas branches, except in Spain, Greece, Austria and Denmark where a small charge has to be made because of Government rules. Commission is generally based on a percentage of the cheque's value and can range from ½% to 1½%. In a small village you are usually at the mercy of the local – and possibly only – bank. They may take advantage of their monopoly and hike up the charges.

In some countries, the commission is based on the number of cheques cashed. If you are cashing lots of small cheques, this can work out to be very expensive. Countries which operate this way include: Austria, Belgium, Denmark, Italy, Malta, Norway,

Visa	American Express	Thomas Cook	Nat West	CitiCorp	Bank America
US Dollars	US Dollars	US Dollars	Sterling	US Dollars	US Dollars
Canadian Dollars	Canadian Dollars	Canadian Dollars		Sterling	Deutsche Mark
Sterling	Sterling*	Sterling		Deutsche Mark	Sterling
German Marks	German Marks	Australian Dollars		Japanese Yen*	French Francs
French Francs*	Dutch Guilder*	French Francs			
Swiss Francs	Swiss Francs	Hong Kong Dollar*			
Japanese Yen	Japanese Yen	Japanese Yen			
Spanish Pesetas	*Servicing Agreements*	Swiss Francs*			
Hong Kong Dollar	Saudi Riyal	Ecu			
Australian Dollar	Ecu	Spanish Peseta†			
Portuguese Escudos					

* Joint venture with baking group
† To be launched summer 1986

Holland and Sweden. So try and take large value cheques to these countries.

Retailers should not charge any form of commission when you use the cheques to pay for goods or services. However, you may lose out by getting a poorer exchange rate than the local bank quotes.

How to Use Them

You'll need to show your passport when cashing a travellers cheque. It can be a bit of a nuisance carrying this valuable document around with you, but fraud and forgery are rife. Bank cashiers are trained to be on the lookout for potential thieves. If you don't come armed with your I.D. you'll probably walk away cashless.

Refund Facility

The biggest plus with travellers cheques is the refund facilities they offer when they are lost or stolen. If a disaster strikes the major travellers cheque issuers will offer you a so-called instant refund service and you should get your money replaced quickly. Unfortunately, not all issuers provide the same level of refund service, so try to check this out prior to purchase.

Only one in every two hundred and fifty travellers lose their cheques or have them stolen. Still, do take sensible precautions. The most important thing is to make a note of the cheque numbers and to keep this tucked away safely separate from the cheques themselves. All issuers now give you a purchase receipt stating the key details. This acts as proof of purchase and will speed up the refund service, if necessary.

When you buy the cheques, ask for a list or booklet with the addresses of the bank or agents abroad which handle refunds.

If the worst happens, inform the local police straight away and try to get written confirmation from them. Then contact the nearest agent for your particular brand of travellers cheques. Give them a copy of your receipt slip, which will show the nmumbers and confirm that the cheques have not been countersigned.

In some countries, such as the USA and Canada, your refunds can take only a few minutes. Elsewhere you may have to wait 24 hours. If you have lost a large amount of money, you might not get it all back at once. However, the major issuers will make immediate refunds once they have checked out the position. Nat West has the most strongly worded clause in its travellers cheque literature about negligence. It states refunds will be made providing 'the cheques were not handled in an irresponsible manner'.

Large value refunds have to be confirmed by telex. If a thief steals your cheques and forges your signature in the 'counter-signature' box, you will not be involved in any loss.

Getting Your Refund

Issuer	Immediate Amount	Number of Locations
AMEX	open	over 100,000
Thomas Cook	up to £400	over 5,000 Thomas Cook offices some Wagon-Lits and Hertz, plus 100,000 bank branches
VISA	up to £500*	at the 170,000 member banks or outside banking hours at over 60,000 including Western Union, Sheraton Hotels and Europcar
Nat West	up to £250	in excess of 700 agents

*Varies – limit set by issuing bank.

Pros and Cons
(a) Travellers Cheques
Taken at face value, travellers cheques are a good buy. They are relatively cheap, easy to cash and can be replaced if lost or stolen. However, do remember you are paying money up front for this facility – sometimes weeks before you actually spend the money. During this interval, the bank or society from which you bought the travellers cheques has free use of your money. What's more they have charged you for this privilege. You can see why the

40

ravellers cheque business is so profitable. It's hardly surprising hat the advertisements state 'If you have any cheques left over lon't worry – keep them until your next trip, there is no time limit'. After all, it's not every day customers hand over their money and bay a charge for this. In fact, you are giving the travellers cheque ssuer a free loan and being charged for the cheques.

b) Sterling Travellers Cheques

Plus

1. Pound is acceptable around the world.

2. If you don't use all the cheques you can use them commission free at home or pay them into your account just like cash.

3. You have security and peace of mind as any losses will be refunded.

Minus

1. Sterling is not popular in the USA.

2. You may get a poorer rate of exchange than if you switched into foreign currency at home.

3. You pay commission twice – on purchase and when you when you cash them.

c) Foreign Currency Travellers Cheques

Plus

1. You know exactly how much you have to spend.

2. Quicker to cash at local bank than sterling.

3. If sterling falls, you will be insured against a loss.

4. Useful means of taking large sums abroad as cash.

5. Once counter-signed many countries treat them as cash.

Minus

1. If the pound rises, then you don't benefit.

2. You pay commission twice on any cheques brought back to the UK.

3. Some problems arise with travellers cheques issued by smaller banks. There may be difficulties in getting them cashed or obtaining a refund in the event of a loss.

Chapter 5
EURO MONEY

"Darling, do you think we will ever be able to afford FREE BANKING?"

In 1968 a number of Western European banks banded together to start up the Uniform Eurocheque system. As the name implies, the idea was to provide a system for cashing cheques in Europe. Initially, Eurocheques could only be used as a way of getting cash from banks, but now they can be used for goods and services in shops and hotels as well.

The British banks studiously ignored the Uniform Eurocheque system for years and stuck with the Eurocheque Encashment card. This was an overseas version of a cheque guarantee card and could be used to support British cheques at European banks. The Uniform Eurocheque system proved very popular and the British banks, led by the Midland, have now joined the Continental system. Uniform Eurocheques look a bit like a cross between travellers cheques and ordinary cheques. They are printed on high security paper.

Acceptability

Eurocheques can be used in 39 different countries at over 200,000 bank offices. What's more, over 4.5 million shops, garages, hotels, restaurants and other outlets accept them as readily as cash. In 1985 1,744,000 Eurocheques were processed in the UK alone, which were worth nearly £100 million. They can be used in the following countries:

- All European countries

- Iron curtain countries, Bulgaria, Czechoslovakia, Hungary, Poland, Rumania, USSR, Yugoslavia

- Plus Albania, Egypt, Israel, Finland, Lebanon, Cyprus, Madeira, Canary Islands, Morocco, Tunisia and Iceland.

The Eurocheques are not widely accepted in the USSR and Egypt, so travellers should take other forms of 'holiday money'.

How the System Works

1. The cheques come either in books of 10 or are supplied loose. Your account number is printed on each one in the normal way.
2. You will be given a Eurocheque card which looks a little like an ordinary cheque guarantee card, but has the EC symbol in one corner. This card guarantees that the cheque will be honoured up to a maximum of £100 or the rough equivalent in foreign currency.
3. You write out the cheque in the local currency of the country you are visiting for any amount up to the maximum limit. You fill in the rest of the details in exactly the same way as with an ordinary cheque. In the Eastern block you make out the cheque in US dollars.
4. The cheque will be debited to your account in the same way as a domestic cheque. As you have made out the cheque in a foreign currency your account will be debited by the equivalent sum in sterling based on the exchange rate applicable on the day the cheque arrives back in this country.
5. If you are cashing a few cheques then in theory all you need is your Eurocheque card. In practice, many foreign banks insist on seeing your passport – so take it with you just in case.
6. There is no limit to the number of Eurocheques you can use to complete a purchase. If you want to cash more than three cheques in a bank at the same time however, then take some form of ID such as your passport.

Below are the current amounts guaranteed in local currency for the most popular countries. These are all approximately the equivalent of £100, but rounded up. The guaranteed figure is based on the 'international' value of 300 Swiss Francs.

Eurocheque Guarantee Ceilings

Country	Currency	Maximum Limit Guaranteed
Austria	Schilling	2,500
Belgium	Belgian Franc	7,000
France	French Franc	1,000
West Germany	Mark	400
Greece	Drachma	17,000
Italy	Lira	250,000
Malta	Maltese Pound	60
Morocco	French Franc	1,000
Norway	Krone	1,000
Portugal	Escudo	20,000
Spain/Canary Isles	Peseta	20,000
Switzerland	Swiss Franc	300
Tunisia	Dinar	100
Yugoslavia	Dinar	20,000

Where to Buy

You can't just walk into a bank and buy Eurocheques. You have to apply to your bank manager for a Eurocheque guarantee card. These are not given out carte blanche. The bank manager vets every application and only credit worthy customers will be given one. Each book of Eurocheques contains 10 cheques, each of which can be cashed for £100. So the bank has to feel that you are good for £1,000. If you have a joint account, apply for two guarantee cards. Anyone with several accounts should choose which account they want to use.

You can get an application form at your local branch. Try to allow a couple of weeks for the card to be printed up and posted to you.

What It Costs

Eurocheques are provided free of charge. However, the guarantee card costs up to £3.50 each year as our table shows. The charge varies from bank to bank. Most cards are valid for two years, but you'll find the bank debits your account with the annual fee automatically.

Then there is a commission of 1.25% on the value of the transaction, that's £1.25 per £100 cashed. This is paid to the bank handling the cheque. If you cash a cheque at a foreign bank you may have to pay this commission then and there. If you use the cheques at a shop or hotel then the commission will be knocked off your account back home.

Finally, your own bank charges a handling fee as our table shows. This charge is debited to your account when the cheque is processed. Retailers are not allowed to make any extra charges for handling Eurocheques.

Eurocheque Charges

Banks	Annual Fee	Foreign Bank Fee	Handling Charge (per cheque)
Barclays	£4.00	1.25%	30p
Lloyds	£3.50	1.25%	30p
Midland	£3.50	1.25%	31p
Nat West	£3.50	1.25%	29p
Royal Bank*	£7.00	1.25%	28p
TSB	£3.50	1.25%	30p

*valid for two years

Examples

Suppose you want to write a Eurocheque in Spain. The maximum amount per cheque is 20,000 pesetas:

Cheque	20,000
Plus commission of 1.25% for Spanish bank	250
	20,250 pesetas

The cheque will be sent back to your account in the UK and debited with the sterling equivalent of 20,250 pesetas. If the rate the day it gets back is 200 to the pound, you will have to pay £101.25. Add to this the UK bank handling charge of 30p and the total amount debited to your account will be £101.55p

Sometimes you will have to write out the cheque in US dollars. Eastern block countries plus Turkey, Egypt and Israel normally insist on this. The maximum amount per cheque is US$130:

Cheque	$130
Plus commission 1.25% for the bank handling the cheque	1.62
	$131.62

Your own bank will convert $131.62 to sterling. If the rate is $1.40 to the pound, you will pay £94.02. Add the handling charge of 30p and your account will be debited with £94.32.

Comparisons with other forms of holiday money:

Suppose you buy £100 pesetas in England at 200 to the pound at a typical commission cost of £1. Interest for two weeks on £100 at 10% is equivalent to around 40p. Total cost works out to £101.40. Comparing this to the Eurocheque example of £101.55 there isnot much in it. Though remember, you also have to take account of the annual fee of around £3.50 for the Eurocheque card.

Pros

1. In Europe can be used to cash cheques at banks and used to pay for goods and services in a wide range of outlets.

2. The cheque can be made out for the exact amount you require.

Cons

1. The cheques are relatively expensive, especially if you write lots of small cheques.

2. You take a risk, (which might also work in your favour), of the sterling/foreign currency rate moving against you on your return home.

49

3. They are safer than cash and have limited thief appeal, provided you keep the guarantee card separate from the Eurocheques

4. Your money is not tied up or used until you actually need it. Eurocheques are usually debited to your account a few days after use so you can count on a period of 'interest free credit'.

5. There is no limit on the number of cheques you can use to pay for a single bill.

6. You can use them to pay deposits in foreign currency. For example if you want to rent a flat abroad and the owner wants a deposit, you can simply post him a Eurocheque. This is a much cheaper method of making overseas payment than either a bank transfer or telex.

3. If the cards or the cheques are lost or stolen when you are abroad, you cannot normally get a replacement until you return home.

Cash Points

Customers of the Midland, Clydesdale and National Westminster Bank can use their uniform Eurocheque cards to draw cash from a limited number of machines in Europe. There are about 700 cash dispensers in use in Spain now and networks in Britain and Europe. Germany and Portugal will add a further 1,000 machines by this summer. The numbers are growing. The plan is to install around 10,000 machines across the nineteen participating countries, all of which can be accessed with a local Eurocheque card. To take advantage of these cash dispensers you'll need a special personal identification number or PIN from your bank. You can't use the same code as you tap in at home. At present travellers to Spain can withdraw up to 20,000 pesetas per day, that's roughly £100. The machines are open 24 hours a day, 7 days a week, so you can get cash outside normal banking hours. Your local branch will give you a directory of this cash dispenser network.

Use in Britain

The Eurocheques aren't limited to continental Europe. They can be used at home – and come in very useful for families planning a UK holiday. If you want to draw cash from a bank using your cheque guarantee card, you are limited to a maximum of £50 a cheque. But there are no limits with Eurocheques, The sky, or rather your bank balance, sets the limit.

If you buy goods and services using your cheque guarantee card you can only guarantee one cheque for up to £50. With the Eurocheque you can issue as many cheques as you like for up to £100 – so shopkeepers and hoteliers should be much happier accepting Eurocheques.

Another advantage of using the Eurocheque system in this country is that the cost is lower. The 1.25% commission is not charged if they are cashed at your own bank and so long as you qualify for free banking you won't be charged the 30p handling fee. Remember, if you overdraw your account in the quarter you use the Eurocheque then the bank will impose the standard handling fee.

Theft

Do not keep the card and book of cheques in the same handbag or pocket. If the cheques are stolen with the Eurocheque card then the crook can just copy your signature and fool the local bank into parting with the cash.

When you apply for a card, you sign an agreement with the bank. Hidden in the small print is your undertaking to take all possible care of both the cheques and the card. However, if the cheques and the card are stolen, it is unlikely the bank will make you liable for any loss. By law your account cannot be debited with a cheque which does not have your signature. Make sure you don't sign any of the cheques in blank, always wait until you are in front of the person you are paying. If the cheques or card, or both, are stolen, report this immediately to the local police. At the same time you should let your own bank know about the loss as soon as possible. There is no instant replacement available for Euro-cheques, unlike travellers cheques.

Chapter 6
PLASTIC CREDIT

"I bet my DAD'S OVERDRAFT can beat your DAD'S OVERDRAFT"

The advance of the plastic revolution has been uneven. Plastic is king in the United States but a mere pawn in many European countries. For the traveller plastic credit cards have become the ace in the tourist money pack.

Credit cards are issued free and are a handy way of paying for goods or service. You are billed monthly and have the choice of either settling your debt in full or opting to pay the balance over a number of months. You pay interest on the balance which is usually quoted as a certain amount per month. For short term credit it is relatively cheap. The main limitation is that you have to stick to a pre-set spending limit, although you can get this raised for special occasions such as holidays.

Credit Giants

Credit cards are big business. To be successful a piece of plastic has to be acceptable around the world and that's where two international 'umbrella' organisations come in. Together Mastercard and VISA have signed up most of the world's leading banks. They effectively run two parallel international cards systems. They operate clearing systems for participating banks and co-ordinate marketing.

How the UK banks divide up

Mastercard	*Visa*
Clydesdale Bank	Barclays
Lloyds	Trustee Savings Bank
Royal Bank of Scotland	Yorkshire Bank
National Westminster	Bank of Scotland

Northern and Ulster Bank	Co-op Bank
Midland	National Girobank
Bank of Ireland	
Coutts	

In the UK three of the country's largest high street banks clubbed together to form Access, which in turn is linked to Mastercard in the US and Eurocard in Europe. These links give the trio – Lloyds, Midland and National Westminster – the advantage of having their cards accepted in more than four million outlets worldwide.

Barclaycard is owned and operated by Barclays. The card itself has a dual function it acts as both a credit card and cheque guarantee card within the UK. As Barclays is a member of VISA the card can be used in the group's 4.4 million outlets in one hundred and sixty countries.

When you use a credit card abroad the bill is paid in the local currency. The credit card voucher is forwarded to the bank in the UK and the sum you owe is then converted into sterling. The debit is added to your next monthly statement.

With VISA members the process is complicated by the fact that all transactions are switched into dollars before being sent for processing to a VISA centre. They then have to be converted from dollars to sterling so your account can be debited. With two lots of exchange rates involved this can work out expensive, especially as the local bank can choose its own dollar rate.

How Europe is served

Country	VISA	Mastercard
France	216,000	83,000
Spain	202,000	110,000
Italy	77,000	39,000
Northern Europe	40,000	49,000
Western Europe	56,000	60,000
Southern Europe	123,000	71,000

Exchange Rate

On the whole customers get a better rate of exchange with a credit card than other forms of holiday money. That's because it is the credit card issuer which is clinching the foreign currency transaction and as a major currency player it can deal at better rates than an individual. The other point to watch is timing. The crucial exchange rate is the one ruling when the voucher arrives back in the UK, sometimes weeks after you spent the money. In most cases the advantages of up to eight weeks free credit more than outweigh any slippage within that timespan in the value of sterling.

For example, I was in Spain at Christmas. The rate of exchange was 220 pesetas to the pound at the time. I got my Barclaycard statement at the end of January. It had the following entry: Voucher for 4,200 pesetas, Marbella equals £20.

This shows that the rate had dropped to 210 pesetas to the pound by the time the transaction was converted back to sterling. 4,200 pesetas at 220 to the pound is £19.10, so I am 90p worse off. However, I don't have to pay the bill until the end of February, so I have had the free use of the money for two months. This more than makes up for the loss of 90p.

Cash Facility

With an Access card you can usually withdraw £100 or more a day at a Mastercard member bank. Interest starts clocking up the moment the sterling equivalent is charged to your account but there is no commission charge.

VISA issuers allow customers the facility of withdrawing up to £100 per day. They usually insist on checking to make sure you are within your credit limit. There is a fee of 1½% which is added to your cash withdrawal. Then the item is treated just like a regular purchase and you only pay interest if your bill is not settled on the due date.

You can use your credit card to get cash from dispensers around the world. Access holders who bank with Midland or National Westminster can tap into the network run by the Continental banks who run the Eurocheque system. VISA has nearly five and a half thousand machines and hopes to double this by the end of 1985. Nearly 20% of its network is in Spain and just over 10% in France at present.

Insurance

Competition between the credit card companies is hotting up. In a bid to win your loyalty they are bolting on a number of perks to the basic credit line facility. For instance if you book your travel with a credit card then the company will throw in a certain amount of free accident insurance. Keep your sales voucher as proof and contact the company's customer services department if you need to claim.

Card	*Maximum Cover Limit*
Access-Lloyds	£20,000
Access–Midland	£15,000
Access–National Westminster	Nil
Barclaycard	£50,000

Credit Card Bonuses

When you use your credit card to make a purchase that transaction falls within the scope of the Consumer Credit Act. This can prove very helpful.

If the tour operator goes bust
If you bought your holiday with a credit card and the operator goes bust, then the credit card company will refund your money provided the bill was between £100 and £30,000. This applies even if you only paid the deposit for the holiday by credit card provided of course it was more than the £100 floor.

If your credit card is stolen
By law your liability will be limited to £50. In practice provided you report the loss promptly you are unlikely to suffer financially.

No surcharge
You should not be charged a commission when you pay with your credit card. Some foreign retailers do try to pass on the commission which they in turn are charged by the credit card company but if this happens threaten to report them. If this fails, get a full receipt and report the offender once you return home. Insist on a rebate.

Acceptability

In the United States cash is infra dig. Credit cards are preferred, followed by travellers cheques in lieu of dollars. Around the world you'll find the higher the tourist numbers the greater the level of acceptance. Don't expect isolated villages in the middle of nowhere to leap into ecstasy at the sight of your piece of plastic.

One major problem area is garages. Particularly in Italy you may find your credit card greeted with a sneer. Elsewhere they may try to charge you extra. If you are planning a long drive or motoring holiday make sure you have plenty of cash as a back-up.

Advantages

1. Convenience. No need to make any special arrangements before you go away.
2. Time saving. No frustrating hours spent queuing at the local bank for cash.
3. Cost effective. You get up to seven weeks free credit and your savings can be earning interest while you're spending the money overseas.
4. Popular. Accepted in most holiday resorts.

Checklist

- Expiry date. Check card is valid throughout your holiday.
- Spending limit. Ask company to raise this if necessary.
- Paperwork. Keep all receipts and vouchers. Check these with your statement on return home.

Chapter 7

CHARGE IT

"To stop money burning a hole in his pocket, HENRY spends it like WATER ..."

Plastic charge cards are fighting a rearguard battle against the invasion of that upstart the popular credit card. Charge cards as their name suggests are simply a way of paying bills. You receive a monthly account which must be settled straight away. If you don't pay on time you may be charged an extra amount and ultimately forfeit your card. Their main attraction is the absence of pre-set spending limits.

The best known charge cards, sometimes referred to as 'T & E' – travel and entertainment – are American Express and Diners. Unlike credit cards you pay to use these. Both charge a £22.50 annual fee and a £15 joining fee.

American Express

A worldwide company whose staple green card is familiar across the globe. It has more than 1,200 offices and over one million agents. As there is no pre-set spending limit applicants for a green card are carefully screened.

The main disadvantage for travellers using the card abroad is the 1% processing charge which American Express adds to all bills when these are converted back to sterling. There is also the hurdle of the fees involved. Against this American Express offers a range of incentive schemes such as a free bottle of wine at certain restaurants or £20 worth of travellers cheques free if you pay for a holiday with your card. The incentives run for a fixed period and details are included with your monthly bill.

Diners Club

The giant American bank Citicorp, owns Diners Club UK. As with American Express would-be customers are vetted with care. The charges are similar with the 1% processing charge for foreign transactions. In addition, there is a special service charge for late payers of 2% or more.

In an attempt to get its customers to use Diners Club more often, the company offers an incentive called 'dividends'. Each card holder is given a spending target based on previous levels. If you match this then you earn ten dividends that month. Every £25 you overshoot your target clocks up another five dividends. You can then use your dividends to 'buy' goods from the Diners Club Dividends catalogue. For example, a Pierre Cardin wallet 'costs' 400 dividends while a Peugeot 205 GTi can be yours for a mere 110,000 dividends.

Cash in Hand

You can use your Diners Club card to draw up to $1,000 in local currency but you'll end up paying 4% for the privilege. So try not to run out of readies. A cheaper option is to try and locate a branch of Citibank where Diners Club holders will be charge 1% for a loan of up to $1,000

American Express card holders cannot use the piece of plastic to get cash. However, it does act as a cheque guarantee card when used to back up your own cheques and presented at one of the group's offices. This way you can have access to up to £500 over three weeks.

Gold Version

Upmarket charge cards for top wage earners in the £25,000 a year salary bracket are becomingly increasingly popular. These are designed for the frequent traveller and although more expensive than the standard version offer a range of useful facilities.

Upper crust plastic

CARD	SOURCE
American Express Gold	Lloyds, Bank of Ireland, Royal Bank of Scotland, Grindlays, American Express
VISA Premium	Barclays, Bank of Scotland, Robert Fleming/Save & Prosper
Gold Mastercard	Midland

Charges for these gold cards range from American Express which bills customers with a £20 joining fee plus £50 per annum to Midland, which has no enrolment fee and asks for £40 per year.

Special Perks

So what do you get for a gold card, apart from an internationally recognised status symbol to flash around your hotel?

- Automatic overdraft facility at very competitive rate
- Generous travel accident insurance of at least double the £75,000 for ordinary cardholders
- Daily cashing facility of £350 at participating banks
- Higher daily limit for cash dispenser withdrawals – usually £300 or more
- Confirmed hotel reservation service
- Emergency telephone service abroad
- Emergency cash facility of around $5,000
- Additional perks eg Mastercard gold offers a visa and passport renewal service via Thomas Cook. Diners Club has special lounges in certain international airports.

Charge Cards: Pros and Cons

Pluses

1. No pre-set spending limit
2. International recognition
3. Convenient

Minuses

1. Charges for card
2. Additional fees for international transactions
3. Unlike credit cards, there is no limited liability in case of loss or fall back position of being able to claim a refund from the card company if the retailer goes bust.
4. No credit facility on ordinary charge card
5. Smaller number of outlets than some credit cards (see table).

Card Networks

Country	AMEX	%‡	Diners Club	%‡	VISA	%‡	Eurocard	%‡
Andorra	340	1	260	3	800	2	453	1
Austria	7,500	25	8,500	21	9,600	47	9,836	17
Belgium	11,000	37	9,500	20	7,200	20	9,573	37
Denmark	3,500	75	5,000	31	6,400	62	6,400	62
Finland	2,800	34	2,000	100	10,600	54	10,600	54
France	40,000	-20	25,000	0	275,000	14	109,950	31
Germany	40,000	33	35,000	34	25,000	38	34,709	25
Greece	8,200	-5	6,600	9	14,200	29	12,831	—
Iceland	200*		100*		1,500	N.A.	1,428	120
Ireland	3,500*		3,000*		9,000	34	7,891	15
Israel	1,100	-33	4,000	14	8,800	-5	8,953	6
Italy	42,000	-6	30,000	20	75,000	0	39,993	4
Netherlands	9,000	38	7,500	N.A.	7,000	N.A.	6,623	29
Norway	3,700	23	3,550	94	3,400	38	3,400	55
Portugal	3,100	14	3,100	14	8,300	13	8,108	11
Spain	35,000	0	20,000	-9	213,000	42	121,190	10
Sweden	10,300	47	6,000	71	30,000	100	32,048	10
Switzerland	14,700	22	13,000	44	15,000	N.A.	13,679	24
Turkey	N.A.		N.A.		4,900	N.A.	2,928	57
United Kingdom	78,000	30	57,000	14	207,000	-3	217,926	6
Yugoslavia	3,000		N.A.		1,000	N.A.	2,800	55
TOTAL	316,940	10	239,110	16	932,700	17	668,926	15

Notes

1. *In order to maintain consistency at total level, estimates have been made. 2. Figures refer to number of outlets. 3. %‡ represents the percentage increase over the previous year.

Source: Access as at 1984

Chapter 8

GETTING POSTED

"We're giving this free 'T'-shirt to all our new young investors"

National Girobank, the bank in your post office, is easy to over look because it is faceless. You don't often see its name in lights o the high street. In this case, appearances are deceiving. Nationa Girobank, the country's fastest growing bank, already ranks sixt in the league and offers travellers a range of holiday mone services which are virtually unbeatable. 20,000 post offices offe National Girobank services.

Traditional Services

First, let's look at how National Girobank fares when it comes t those banking staples, travellers cheques, foreign currency an credit cards. Thomas Cook sterling travellers cheques are avai able at all post offices but if you want something more exotic it ha to be ordered from National Girobank. You can choose from:

- US dollars
- Canadian dollars
- Australian dollars
- Swiss francs
- Spanish pesetas
- French francs
- German Deutshmarks
- Japanese yen
- Hong Kong dollars
- Dutch guilders

There is a 1% commission charge on all travellers cheques. Girobank customers can order their travellers cheques from home. You simply complete a personal transfer form, specify what currency you want and return this to the bank in an envelope marked 'travel currency section'. Make sure you sign the travellers cheques when you receive them through the post.

If you have any travellers cheques left over on your return, you can send them back to the bank and ask for your account to be credited. Foreign currency cheques will be converted into pounds at the exchange ruling on the day they are received and a 1% charge on this sterling value will be debited as a handling charge.

As for foreign currency, Girobank customers can order a wide range of tourist currencies by post. Remember to allow a week for delivery. There is a 1% service charge. Exotic currencies may take slightly longer to arrive. Leftover foreign notes can be returned and their sterling value minus a 1% handling charge will be credited to your account.

Forty-one post offices offer a comprehensive bureau de change service. They sell foreign currency travellers cheques as well as foreign currency itself. There is a standard 1% commission on all transactions and the exchange rate given is normally similar to that at a high street bank.

Bureaux de Change

Office	Address	Phone No.
Ambleside	Ambleside SSo, Cumbria, LA22 9AA	09663 2180
Bath	25 New Bond St, BA1 1AA	0225 25481
Belfast	Shaftesbury Sq, BT2 7DA	0232 26177
Bournemouth	Post Office Rd, BH1 1AA	0202 28811
Brighton	51 Ship St, BN1 1AA	0273 29292
Broadway	High St, WR12 7DW	038 6 853377
Cambridge	9/11 St Andrews St, CB1 1AA	0223 51212
Canterbury	28 High St, CT1 1AA	0227 63211
Cardiff	The Hayes, 4 Hill St, CF1 2SJ	0222 30531
Chester	2 St John St, CH1 1AA	0244 315566
Chichester	10 West St, PO19 1AA	0243 784251
Dover	65/66 Biggin St, CT16 1BA	0304 202391
Edinburgh	2/4 Waterloo Place, EH1 1AA	031 550 8229

DON'T TRAVEL
FOR
TRAVELLERS
CHEQUES

Thomas Cook
Sterling Travellers Cheques.
Buy them at your local
Post office.

Folkestone	7/9 Bouverie Place, CT20 1AA	0303 55214
Fort William	5 High St, PH33 6AA	0397 2974
Hastings	Cambridge Rd, TN34 1AA	0424 437940
Inverness Bo	14/16 Queensgate, IV1 1AA	0463 34111
Ipswich	Cornhill, IP1 1AA	0473 52660
Keswick	48 Main St, CA12 5JJ	0596 72119
Liverpool	33/34 Whitechapel	051 242 4009
London		
Earl's Court	185 Earl's Court Rd, SW5 9RB	01 370 2841
Gloucester Road	153 Gloucester Rd, SW7 4TB	01 370 2071
King Edward St	London Chief P.O., EC1A 1AA	01 601 9106
Lancelot Place	10 Lancelot Pl, SW7 1DS	01 589 0633
Parliament St	44 Parliament St, SW1A 2LU	01 839 1035
Queensway	118/120 Queensway, W2 6LT	01 229 5257
Regent Street (Lower)	11 Lower Regent St, SW1Y 4LX	01 930 9538
Southampton Row	71 Southampton Row, WC1B 4EY	01 636 4848
Trafalgar Square	24–28 William IV St, WC2H 4DL	01 930 8820
Victoria Street	110 Victoria St, SW1E 5JU	01 834 0509
Manchester Airport	Airport P.O., M22 5NU	061 437 5233
Norwich	Bank Plain, NR2 4AA	0603 614633
Oxford	012/104 St Aldates, OX1 1AA	0865 49211/ 812749
Penzance	113 Market Jew St, TR18 2LB	0736 2464
Perth	South St, PH1 1AA	0738 31444/ 23402
Plymouth	5 St Andrew's Cross, PL1 1AA	0752 665776
Rye	Cinque Ports St, TN31 7AA	07973 3301
Salisbury	24 Castle Street, SP1 1AA	0722 27745
Shrewsbury	8 St Mary's St, SY1 1AA	0743 62925
Stratford Upon Avon	24/26 Bridge St, CV37 6AA	078929 3241
Torquay	Fleet St, TQ1 1AA	0803 213200
York	22 Lendal, YO1 2DA	0904 28901

On the credit card front, Girobank customers are issued with VISA cards. These can be used in the same way as credit cards issued by the other high street banks. In addition up to £100 a day can be withdrawn through the Girobank's system of cash dispensers, known as LINK.

Postcheques
A unique and handy service offered to Girobank customers is

postcheques. These are similar to standard cheques but must be backed up with a Postcheque card, sent free with your first batch. They can be used to withdraw cash in local currency at over 90,000 post offices in thirty-two countries. These include: Austria, Belgium, Cyprus, Denmark, Finland, France, Germany, Gibraltar, Greece, Irish Republic, Israel, Italy, Malta, Morocco, Netherlands, Norway, Portugal, Spain, Sweden, Switzerland, Tunisia, Turkey and Yugoslavia.

Postcheques

How to order:	Send a completed application form, 'Travel by Postcheques' to Girobank's Bootle office. Allow 10 days for delivery
Cost:	Issued free. Flat charge of 50p per cheque used.
Exchange rate:	Tends to be slightly poorer than on travellers cheques but this is balanced by absence of commision charges
Debit:	The sterling equivalent of your transaction plus the 50p is debited from your account back home
Amount:	Varies. Around £65 per cheque
Restrictions:	Few. You can use as many cheques as you like per day. Some countries insist each one is written for a fixed sum.

Sending Money Abroad

The cheapest and easiest method is to transfer money from your Girobank account to the postal Giro account of the person or company overseas. The process can be speeded up by paying £6 for rapid transfer which means the instructions are telexed. Overseas payments can be made to international banks. There is a minimum charge of £2.50 plus any additional fees incurred. Rather than incur these charges, try sending a foreign currency cheque. The cost of this varies but it works out cheaper than going through the normal banking channels. These are available in the currencies of the following countries:

Australia, Austria, Belgium, Canada, Cyprus, Denmark, Finland,

France, Germany, Greece, Hong Kong, India, Ireland, Italy, Japan, Luxembourg, Norway, Portugal, Singapore, South Africa, Spain, Sweden, Switzerland and the USA. If you are sending money elsewhere go for US dollars, they are almost universally acceptable.

Avoid sterling travellers cheques as this can work out very expensive. This will usually involve two whacks of commission and may generate exchange problems at the receiving end.

More Information

Girobank customers who want more information on international services should write to:

> The Manager
> International Services Branch
> National Girobank
> Bootle, Merseyside IR 0AA

If you have an urgent query then telephone 051-993 3330 or telex 627273 GIROB G.

Chapter 9

GOING NATIVE

"I see you can't afford my fee"

If you are planning to buy a home abroad or escape the winter cold, then you'll need access to substantial sums of money. One option is to open a foreign currency account at your local bank. You'll get interest on your money and a cheque book. There are several advantages. First, an investment in a foreign currency can be a good hedge against a fall in the value of the pound. For example, you may buy Spanish pesetas at 200 to the pound two weeks before you go on holiday. When you actually leave, the rate is 150 to the pound. You are therefore 50 pesetas per pound better off than if you had bought the currency just before leaving. Obviously the opposite applies if the peseta stands at 250 to the pound on your departure date. Second, you know exactly where you stand in terms of how much currency you have to spend. This is useful for budgeting and forward planning. Finally, there's the ability to pay foreign bills with a local currency cheque which may be useful. However, you may find difficulty in both cashing cheques and using your cheques to pay for goods and services in shops and restaurants.

The main disadvantage is you'll need a hefty deposit to start such an account. The amount required varies from bank to bank, and from currency to currency. However, £1,000 is the norm on interest paying accounts, though a much higher figure can be required for some types of account.

Added to this are relatively high costs. The charges for running a bank account in a foreign currency are usually higher than on a sterling account. Again, this varies from bank to bank – you may find the charges reduced if you keep a large balance. At Barclays, for example, there is no charge if your average balance is £500 or more, providing you don't need a cheque book. If your balance drops below £500 there is a £5 per quarter charge, less notional interest. A cheque book costs £5 per quarter charge, plus a flat fee of 50p per cheque less notional interest.

Finally, some countries impose restrictions which make it impossible to open an account in their currency overseas.

Foreign Bank Accounts

Here, you open an account with a foreign bank in the local currency. This is useful if you have a financial link with a particular country, such as a flat, villa or time-share. Your own bank can arrange to open an account overseas for you. Many high street banks have subsidiaries around the world particularly in Spain, France and the USA. Opening an account with one of their subsidiaries should involve nothing more complicated than sending a sample signature and an overseas address. If your bank does not have a suitable branch it will arrange to open an account for you with one of its overseas agents. Your branch will supply the foreign bank with the necessary references and signatures. However, you will need to call in at the foreign bank with your passport to arrange for your cheque book. It often makes more sense to have an account with a foreign bank, rather than sticking to a subsidiary of your British one. That way your cheques will be easily accepted.

You can take as much money as you like out of the UK but there may be restrictions on how much you can bring into the foreign country of your choice. Do check in advance. If you don't you could find your money frozen overseas. In Spain, for example, you may have to operate two accounts. A domestic one for any money you get locally, from which you can pay immediate bills, and an external account, for money you want to move in and out of the country.

Cheque Cashing Arrangements Overseas

A cheque cashing arrangement with a local foreign bank will mean you can cash your own cheques at a specified bank abroad. You don't have to open a separate bank account. Simply tell your bank how long you'll need the arrangement. You can even arrange for a third party, for example, your husband or wife, to cash cheques as well.

It's easy to set this up. Call at your branch and give them an example of your signature. If you know of a bank abroad in the right locality you can nominate it. Otherwise, your bank will choose the nearest one for you. Your bank will send your details to the foreign bank and fix a cash limit. For example, you may need up to £50 a day, or £500 a week. You will need to take your passport with you when you want to cash a cheque.

It will take a couple of weeks to set up the arrangement, so talk to your bank about a month before your departure date. A typical bank will charge you £10 plus postage, but this does vary. If the foreign bank is a subsidiary then you may be able to cash your cheques for free. Otherwise, you'll pay commission each time you cash a cheque, usually around 1%.

Foreign Transfers and Payments

There may be occasions when you want to send money abroad. Perhaps to make a down payment on a flat or villa, or to help bail out an offspring who has run out of money on the continent. Sometimes hotels ask independent travellers for a deposit to confirm the booking. Here's the options:

1. **Uniform Eurocheque:** For European and some North African countries. Simply send the cheque with a covering letter (see Chapter 4).

2. **International Money Order:** This is issued by Barclays Bank, but you don't have to have an acount with them to buy them. They can be issued in sterling or US dollars and are pre-signed drafts. They can be bought over the counter at branches and paid for by cash, cheque or by debiting your Barclays account. The bank gives you the money order and you send it off to the overseas payee. They can be issued for amounts of up to £500 or US $1,000. The charge for both is just £2 and a prompt refund is obtainable should it be lost, stolen, damaged or destroyed.

3. **Foreign Drafts:** All banks issue these in a variety of currencies. They are drawn either on the branch of your bank

overseas or one of its agents. They can be issued in sterling or foreign currency. There is generally a minimum charge or £5 or £7.50 and a maximum charge of £30. The bank will give you the foreign draft and this can be sent direct to the overseas payee. You cannot stop payment on a foreign draft and life gets complicated if it's lost or stolen. It can be some time before you get your money back.

4. **International Payments or Transfers:** These are instructions to an agent abroad to pay a fixed sum in a specified currency. The money can be paid to a bank account or handed over to the specified individual at a branch of the bank abroad. Normally it takes a few days for the money to arrive. Charges are similar to those on foreign drafts but the overseas bank will add a handling charge.

5. **Telegraphic or Express Transfers:** This is the fastest way of getting money abroad. The instructions are sent by a telex or cable. You can credit an account or the money can be handed over in person to an individual, provided he or she can identify themselves. This is a particularly useful method if money is needed urgently for someone stranded abroad. Once again the charges will be 25p per £100, though the minimum charge is likely to be higher at £10 or £15 with a maxium of £30. The foreign bank will also make a charge.

6. **Overseas Payment through Post Offices:** (See Chapter 8)

7. **International Gift Bonds:** You may have enjoyed a pleasant holiday in Australia, New Zealand or Canada and want to thank the people you stayed with. Or you may have relatives or friends in these countries to whom you want to send birthday or Christmas presents. Research shows that two and a half million people send gifts by parcel post to these three countries. Thomas Cook has recently launched a gift bond scheme which is an excellent way of sending a present to someone overseas. At the moment, they can only be issued in Australian, New Zealand and Canadian dollars. However, there are plans to extend the service to other countries. The vouchers are available in multiples or 5, 10 and 20 dollars and

can be exchanged at a large number of stores in the three countries concerned. They can be bought from a wide range of retailers in the UK including Thomas Cook and W. H Smith.

Expatriates

If you are planning to emigrate to another country or work abroad for a couple of years, one of your top priorities must be your banking arrangements. All too often, expatriates think they will be able to open a bank account overseas in the same way as they can in Britain. They are in for a shock. Banking in America, Canada and many other countries is carried on in quite a different way from the UK.

Visit your own branch manager as soon as you have made definite arrangements to move overseas. He will be able to make arrangements in advance which will ease the transition. National Westminster has just launched the Red Carpet Executive Service, for those hot-footing it to the US. Its main attraction is that everything is set up before you leave home. Simply give your bank manager a letter from your employer giving details of your job, pay and length of stay. In return, you'll be given a contact in America. Everything will be ready when you arrive – an interest bearing current account, an agreed overdraft line of credit, a VISA credit card, a car purchase loan (an American variation on the mortgage theme), a cash card plus a range of savings accounts. This gets round the problem many people run into of not being able to get their hands on money deposited for weeks until their bank back home has verified their signature.

Chapter 10

MIX'N MATCH

"*The number of people showing an interest in my savings has increased by FIFTY PER CENT over the last two years ...*"

Holidaymakers going abroad have never had such a wide choice of ways of paying for goods and services when travelling. Quite frankly with so many options it can be difficult to work out the best method.

The simple truth is that there is no *one* best way. Most travellers will find it pays to take their money with them in several different forms. The days when travellers cheques alone would cater for holidaymakers needs are gone.

Credit and charge cards

Good points: 1. You don't have to organize anything in advance
2. You aren't dependent on local banks
3. You can splurge now and pay later.

Drawbacks: 1. You can't use them as widely in most European countries as you can in the UK
2. Garages in many countries won't take them
3. If your card is lost or stolen it is difficult or impossible to get a replacement.

VERDICT: Best buy for purchases, with no commission to pay and good exchange rates, can be difficult using the cash withdrawal facility on Access and Visa in some banks.

Foreign Cash

Good points:
1. Convenient – no queuing up at banks to draw out cash
2. You know exactly how much spending power you have – currency fluctuations won't hit you.

Drawbacks:
1. High commission charge usually minimum of 1%
2. No instant replacement service
3. Some countries limit the amount you can take in and bring out.

VERDICT: Take say £50 in foreign cash to tide you over for the first few days – make sure you take on holiday insurance so you can claim for the loss when you get home – best place to buy it is in the banks domiciled in the country you plan to visit.

Foreign Currency Travellers Cheques

Good points:
1. You know exactly how much spending power you have and won't be hit by currency fluctuations
2. You don't have to pay commission when cashing them abroad
3. Good replacement value providing you buy cheques issued by one of the top companies.

Drawbacks:
1. Unreliable refund arrangements if you buy cheques issued by local banks rather than the big companies
2. Most banks charge more when issuing foreign currency cheques

VERDICT: Best buy if you are going to the USA, can also be good value in some European countries, but make sure you buy cheques issued by a big name.

Postcheques

Good points:
1. Cheap – no charge when buying them and only 50p levy when the transaction is debited to your account
2. There are often more post offices than banks in European countries and they are invariably open for longer hours.

Drawbacks:
1. Cheques have a top limit of approx. £65

VERDICT:
A useful and cheap way of financing holiday spending but can't be used as the only method – be prepared to face long queues in post offices in some countries.

Sterling

Good points:
1. Convenient – you can cash sterling bank notes almost anywhere in Europe
2. No commission charged for converting sterling into local currency by most banks
3. A good stand-by where there's a flourishing currency black market or for Eastern European hard-currency shops

Drawbacks:
1. Risky as you are vulnerable to theft or loss
2. Normally you will get a less attractive exchange rate than for travellers cheques.

VERDICT:
Carry small amounts of sterling with you – you might need it if your flight home is delayed. However, if you are planning a trip to one of the Eastern bloc countries it is useful in the hard currency shops.

Sterling Travellers Cheques

Good points:
1. Convenient for Europe – always easy to cash
2. You will get a good refund service if the cheques are lost or stolen

3. Buy them at one of the building societies that allow customers to buy cheques commission free and you've got a reasonable buy for your money.

Drawbacks:
1. Most places charge a 1% commission when you buy and you pay another commission when you sell which makes them expensive
2. Not much use in America and you might have trouble cashing them
3. You might end up with a poor exchange rate if you cash them at shops, hotels and restaurants

VERDICT: Convenient and safe, but quite pricey – not suitable for the USA, but best bet for Eastern bloc countries.

Uniform Eurocheques

Good points:
1. Simple to use – you can write them in local currency
2. Convenient – can be used to pay for goods and services, so cuts out queueing at local banks
3. The network of cash machines in Eurocheque system is expanding fast

Drawbacks:
1. Expensive to use, particularly if you are cashing cheques for small amounts
2. Widely in Northern Europe, but less so in Southern Europe.

VERDICT: A convenient way of organizing holiday spending money, but quite pricey and until the system becomes accepted in all European countries it cannot replace other systems completely.

Chapter 11

EMERGENCY STATIONS

TICKETS

The arrival of our Rail cards has been delayed. We regret any inconvenience caused...

A little advance planning can make all the difference to the success of your holiday or trip abroad. You may not be able to control the weather, but you can at least ensure there are no major storm clouds on the financial horizon.

Passport

As soon as you book your holiday, check your passport to make sure it is still valid. Every year thousands of holidaymakers end up queuing at passport offices or post offices a few days before the departure date just to get this vital document. If you are caught on the hop with an out-of-date passport, it's not a total disaster. You can get a British Visitor's passport over the counter from any post office. It's only available for holidaymakers and won't cover business travel. You need some proof of your identity such as a birth certificate, doctor's medical card, or, if you are a pensioner, a pension book is quite acceptable. The passport lasts for a year and costs £7.50, (£11.25 if a spouse is included).

If you want a full passport, make sure you apply at least a month in advance. The average waiting time is three weeks. During the peak time, that's March, it can take longer for applications to be processed. The 30 page passport costs £15, (£22.50 if your spouse is included). For jetsetters and export salesmen there is a special bumper 94 page passport which costs £30 (£45.00 if the spouse is included).

The Passport Office steadfastly refuses to acknowledge the equality of women – as wives who hold joint passports will find to their cost if they want to travel on their own. For while the husband can use the passport if he is travelling alone, the wife is not able to use it if she is going solo.

If you are just planning to go abroad for a weekend, then the British Excursion Document available over-the-counter at the post office could fit the bill. The cost is £2. You'll need a photograph and must sign it straight away. It covers a maximum stay of 60 hours abroad.

1986 is the last year you will be able to buy the traditional British passport. In 1987 we switch over to the European version. Ireland and Denmark have already started issuing their citizens with the new European version. The new Euro-style passport has EUROPEAN COMMUNITY written across the top – and then the traditional 'UNITED KINGDOM OF GREAT BRITAIN AND NORTHERN IRELAND' underneath.

Protect Your Home

If you want to avoid a visit from the light fingered brigade the secret is to give the impression you are still at home. Burglars prefer empty houses and look for obvious signs that the home-owner is away. Here are a few useful tips:

- Cancel the milk and newspapers.
- Leave a key with a neighbour who can check the house every few days. You might consider adding an address or phone number where you can be reached.
- Arrange for someone to mow the lawn and/or leave a car parked in the driveway.
- Invest in good quality security locks. Make sure all doors and windows are firmly bolted before you leave.
- Timer-activated switches on lights, radios can be a very good way of making it look as though someone is in the house.
- Do not leave valuable possessions lying around the house. Store them in a safe place, possibly even your bank for your own peace of mind.

Forward planning

1. Carry your own basic first aid kit – aspirin, bandages, also any prescription drugs and necessary personal health information.

2. Travel as light as you can. You don't really need to take expensive jewellery on holiday. It's best to leave it at home or in the bank vaults. If you do take expensive cameras, fur coats or jewellery make sure they are covered under the all-risks section of your household insurance policy as your travel policy is unlikely to be sufficient. Don't pack valuables in your suitcase – on my last trips through Heathrow it was obvious that someone had looked through my luggage, even though it was locked.

3. Carry only a small amount of cash when you go abroad. If it's lost or stolen you won't be able to get it replaced until you get home.

4. Order your travellers cheques and foreign currency a couple of weeks before the departure date.

5. Make sure your passport and visas are up to date – if you realise at the last minute that your passport is out-of-date, you can get a temporary one over the counter at the post office. If you are going to an exotic spot, when you book check whether you'll need vacinations or injections. Have them done well before the departure date.

6. Keep a separate list of your travellers cheques serial numbers.

7. Make sure your credit cards have not expired and leave any unnecessary ones at home. A local store credit card won't do you much good in Spain! Keep a separate record of your credit card numbers.

8. Make sure you know the address and phone number of your bank.

9. Don't be tempted to cut costs by not taking out holiday insurance cover. It's bound to be the one year that disaster strikes.

On Your Way

- Keep your valuables with you. Check occasionally you've still got everything, especially when you have been jostled in a crowd.
- Lock all your luggage.
- Do not put your home address on the luggage label on the outward journey. Thieves regularly watch airports to get addresses of possible empty houses.

- A money belt can be a useful way of carrying your money around.

In the Hotel
- Locate fire exits.
- Lock your hotel room whether you are there or not.
- Keep the room key with you or leave it at the hotel desk. Thieves pick up a lot or room keys from restaurant tables and pool-side deck chairs.
- Do not leave 'make up this room early' sign on the door. It tells everyone you have gone out. The maid will still come in to clean the room anyway.
- Make use of the hotel safe or deposit boxes for any special valuables.

In the Resort
A cast-iron way of ruining your holiday is to have all your money, cards, valuables, passport stolen. True, eventually you'll be able to get everything replaced, but the time-consuming queueing and trips to banks, embassies and so on will spoil even the best holiday. So, never keep all your valuables in one place. A golden holiday rule is to spread valuables among the different members of the party. Other things to watch for are:

- Periodically check your cards and cheques to make sure you still have them.
- Don't make hasty exits – give yourself time to make sure you have collected all your belongings.
- Coat pockets, hip pockets and handbags are especially vulnerable to theft. Men should use front trouser pockets or inside jacket pockets.
- Women suffer the majority of thefts because their purses are generally in public view. Try to avoid handbags with shoulder straps and don't leave your bag unattended.
- If you use credit cards, make sure you get the right one back. If possible keep the card in view while it is being processed. This will prevent a sales person making an extra unauthorized copy.

- Ask for the carbon copy when you use your credit card. Then no one can transfer the information, including your signature, on to a blank card.
- Make sure you know the dates of any local bank holidays and remember that banking hours vary from country to country (see Chapter 13).

Chapter 12

LOST AND FOUND

*"Apparently its merely a question of getting the
right inks ..."*

It will never happen to me! Well, it probably won't, but research shows that around one in every 250 people will lose their hard earned cash on holiday. So it is just as well to be prepared.

You don't have to report every loss or theft to the police. However, if it is a question of getting a refund or replacement, or making an insurance claim, then it is best to tell them. In a busy holiday resort, don't be surprised if they show little interest or sympathy. After all, they probably see hundreds of similar cases every week. Still, try and get a written loss report as confirmation. Insurance companies like to see this report. If the police won't co-operate, ask the hotel manager or the resort representative instead.

Travellers Cheques

If you lose your travellers cheques, you should be able to get them replaced within 24 hours. All the major issuers operate a refund service. Pick up a list of foreign agents when you buy the cheques. Contact the nearest refund office and make sure you have a list of the numbers and the purchase receipt. Remember to keep the receipt separate from the cheques.

Plastic Cards

Provided you let the card company know about your loss, you won't be liable for any bills run up by the thief. However, it will be virtually impossible to get replacement for bank credit cards while you are abroad.

1. **Access:** If you lose your card, go to the nearest bank displaying the Mastercard or Eurocard sign. They will notify Access for you. If you can't find one, ring Access direct – you will have to pay for the call.

2. **Barclaycard:** Find the nearest bank with a VISA sign and they will handle the notification. Failing that, ring Barclaycard direct – they will accept a reverse charge call.

3. **American Express:** Inform the nearest office or agent, or ring the company direct. You will not be liable for any misuse provided you tell the company immediately. It is normally possible to get a replacement card with a new number within 24 hours. If you lose all your documents, they will provide you with temporary identification. They will also tell the other card companies of any card loss or theft, help you to make alternative travel arrangements and send a message on your behalf to any one person anywhere.

4. **Diners Club:** If you lose your Diners Club card you should report it immediately to either the nearest Diners Club office, a Citibank branch or by ringing their Farnborough centre telephone number. You can protect yourself from loss by paying a special £1.50 premium, or you can take out their special insurance scheme. You should be able to get a replacement card within 48 hours if the card is lost or stolen – it will be mailed to whatever address you specify.

5. **Eurocards/Eurocheques:** You should tell your own bank as soon as possible. They will normally not be replaceable while you are abroad.

Cash

Cash can't be replaced straight away. However, if you have taken out a holiday insurance policy, you will eventually get most of it back. You'll need a police report as evidence. If you need cash sent to you in an emergency, the best thing is to enlist the help of the local bank. You will need to take your passport – hence the importance of keeping this separate from your cash. Most banks in the UK have a central emergency cash section with their own telex facilities. You should ask the foreign bank to cable this central office. Typical details they will need are:

> Your full name
> Bank name
> Branch address
> Account number
> Amount you need
> Name and address of foreign bank

It should be possible for the money to be with you within 24 hours. This will be an expensive exercise as you will have to pay two lots of charges, your own bank's and the foreign bank's. possible choose a large branch in the place you are standed a they will probably have more knowledge of emergency pro cedures and better facilities. Your own bank should be able to give you a leaflet setting out full details of how to get emergency cash so you ask for this before you depart.

It may be simpler and cheaper to contact your own branch direct. This will almost certainly mean a telephone call as very few branch offices have a telex machine of their own. If you know someone in the bank, ask for them as it will ease the problem of identification. You can always ask a local bank to ring your own branch for you. They can then liaise on the best way of sending money to you. You will need your passport for identification. Expect to pay two lots of bank charges.

Embassies and Consulates
If you find yourself without money or passport, then the British Embassy or Consulate is there to help you. They will certainly provide you with a temporary passport or travel papers. However, they have no legal obligation to lend you any money. Whether they will or not depends very much on how well you can establish your bona fides.

Addresses of British Embassies Abroad in some popular holiday spots

France
35 Rue du Faubourg St Honoré
75383 Paris Cedex 08

Greece
1 Ploutarchou Street
Athens 139

Ireland
33 Merrion Road
Dublin 4

Italy
VIA XX Settembre 80A
00187 Rome

Portugal
Rua de S Domingos à Lapa, 35–39
1296 Lisbon Codex

Spain
Calle de Fernando el Santo 16
Madrid 4

Switzerland
Thunstrasse 50
3005 Berne

USA
3100 Massachusetts Avenue NW
Washington DC 20008

Key Telephone Numbers
In an emergency, you are going to have to make a number of telephone calls. If you have to find the right number to ring, the amount of time and hassle this will involve will double. Below is a list of useful phone numbers. I have also left space for you to fill in your own details, which you can take on holiday with you. Hopefully you won't have to use them!

Access	0702-35211 Card No ....
Barclaycard	0604-21288 Card No ....
	(reverse charge)
Thomas Cook	0733–502995 – Europe
	(reverse charge)
	974-5696 – America
	(reverse charge)
AMEX	01-222-9633 Card No ....
Diners Club	0252-516261 Card No ....
Travellers Cheques	Nos ....
	No. to report loss ....
Own Bank/Branch	Phone No ....
	Your Ac/No ....
Passport No.	....
Eurocheque Card No.	....

"Personally I've never been able to save enough to earn anything ..."

Your best bet is to spend all your foreign currency while you are abroad. But if you do have some left over when you get back to Britain – your local bank might change it back to sterling, though you will have to pay another commission fee – usually 1%. It is unlikely that anyone will be prepared to buy any small coins that you have left over – our table shows the smallest coins that the National Westminster bank will change – and other institutions are likely to take a similar stand. Barclays will buy back silver coins only. But remember that you will get a penal exchange rate for coins compared to notes.

You should also avoid bringing back large denomination notes as they often incur unfavourable exchange rates. Again the table show which notes you should not bring back to the UK. Make sure you sell back your notes and coins to your own bank – many now charge extra commission to non-customers.

Switching Back to Sterling

Country	Smallest coin exchangeable	Notes given unfavourable exchange rate
Austria	5 schilling	not applicable
Belgium	5 Francs	not applicable
Canada	25 cents	$1,000, 100, 50
Denmark	1 krone	not applicable
Finland	1 Markka	FMK 500
France	1 Franc	not applicable
Germany (West)	1 Mark	not applicable

Country	Smallest coin exchangeable	Notes given unfavourable exchange rate
Greece	10 Drachma	Dr. 1,000
Holland	1 Florin	not applicable
Ireland (Eire)	5 pence	IR£100
Italy	100 Lire	Lit 100,000, 50,00
Malta	Not purchased	not applicable
Norway	1 Krone	not applicable
Portugal	5 Escudos	ESC 5,000, 1,000
Spain	25 Pesetas	Ptas 5,000
Sweden	1 Krona	Skr 10,000, 1,000
Switzerland	1 Franc	not applicable
Turkey	Not purchased	LT 10,000, 5,000
USA	5 cents	not applicable
Yugoslavia	Not purchased	Din 1,000, 500

Source: National Westminster

The icing on the cake for millions of tourists returning home after a two week holiday in the sun is the opportunity to buy duty free drinks, cigarettes and gifts. The amount you can bring back into Britain without paying any duty depends on whether you have been to a country in the European Economic Community or not.

Your Just Allowance

Adults buying goods in a non-EEC country or a duty-free shop can bring back one litre of spirits, or two litres of fortified or sparkling wines plus two litres of still table wine. Wine lovers who do not buy spirits or fortified or sparkling wine can bring in a total of four litres of table wine. Those who buy their alcohol in a shop in the EEC can bring in one and a half litres of spirits *or* three litres of fortified or sparkling wine plus five litres of wine. If you don't buy any of these you can boost your table wine to eight litres.

Until May of last year you were not allowed to mix allowances. This meant that if you bought a bottle of spirits on the plane or boat, your wine allowance was restricted to just two litres, regardless of whether it was bought in a shop in an EEC country, or a duty free area. Now travellers can mix allowances and bring in duty free spirit bought on the plane, boat or at the airport, plus four litres of wine bought in an EEC shop.

Adults can bring in up to 200 cigarettes duty free each, or 300 if these are bought in a shop in an EEC country. There are generous allowances for beer too – you can bring back up to 500 litres of beer. The only problem is how to carry it!

Of course, you are perfectly free to bring in more than the stated allowances, but you should declare it and will have to pay extra duty. Goods up to a total value of £28 can be brought in non-EEC countries and duty free shops and up to a value of £207 from shops in EEC countries.

Who's in the EEC

The following countries are members of the EEC: Belgium, Britain, Denmark, France, Greece, Ireland, Italy, Luxembourg, Netherlands, Portugal, Spain and West Germany.

There is a duty free snag awaiting travellers who are heading for the Canary Islands this summer. Even though the Islands are part of Spain and Spain joined the EEC at the start of 1986, the Canaries have their own tax regulations and the Community's higher allowances do not apply there. So for duty-free purposes, the Canaries will be regarded as being outside the EEC. Travellers will only be able to bring back the lower allowances. The same lower allowances applies to travellers going to Gibraltar and Andorra, but not to the Balaeric Islands, or Madeira and the Azores.

How to Complain

If your holiday didn't live up to expectations, your insurance company won't pay out on your claim, or the bank charges an exorbitant commission rate for foreign currency – you should fight for your rights. The secret of a successful complaint is talking to the organization or person with the power to give you redress.

Insurance

If the insurance company won't pay out on your claim, and you think they are in the wrong, first write to the chief general manager at head office. If this does not bring a satisfactory solution, get in touch with:

> The Association of British Insurers
> Aldermary House
> Queen Street
> London EC4 (Tel. 01-248 4477)

If the insurer belongs to one of the two arbitration schemes listed below you can ask them to investigate your claim. The schemes are:

> Insurance Ombudsman Bureau
> 31 Southampton Row
> London WC1 (Tel. 01-242 8613)

> Personal Insurance Arbitration Service (PIAS)
> 75 Cannon Street
> London EC4H 5BH (Tel. 01-236 8761)

If you are unlucky enough to have picked up an illness on holiday which lies dormant and only appears once you are back in the UK, you wont be covered by holiday insurance policies. The rule is that you are only covered for medical expenses while you are actually abroad. Similarly if you have a skiing accident which requires physiotherapy once you get back to the UK, you will find that too is not covered by your holiday insurance policy.

Bank

If you have a complaint about the way your bank has treated you, first complain loudly to someone in the branch. No luck, then write to the head office. Finally, ask the banking ombudsman to investigate your complaint. The address is:

> Banking Ombudsman
> Citadel House
> 5/11 Fetter Lane
> London EC4A 1BR (Tel. 01-583 1395)

Holiday

The Association of British Travel Agents (ABTA) has drawn up a code of conduct which is designed to protect the holidaymaker and make sure complaints are dealt with quickly and fairly. So it's a good idea to use a tour operator or travel agent which is an ABTA member. This code of conduct covers last minute cancellations by the tour operator, alterations, surcharges, overbooking and booking conditions.

If you are dissatisfied with your holiday, your first step is to complain to the resort representative. Then, take up the complaint with the travel agent when you get home. If this still does not work you can write to ABTA which runs an arbitration scheme. The address is:

> Association of British Travel Agents
> 53/54 Newman Street
> London W1P 4AH (Tel. 01-637 2444)

COUNTRY GUIDES

"That's the trouble with the *HONG KONG DOLLAR*, an hour or so after using up your supply you feel like spending some more ..."

Austria

Currency: Schilling   100 Groschen = 1 Austrian Schilling
Exchange Rate: £1 = 23.4 schillings
Currency Retrictions: You cannot take out more that S15,000 (approx £600)
Banking Hours: 8–12.30pm, 1.30–3.00pm, late opening Thursday up to 5.30pm, closed Saturdays
National Holidays: Jan 1, 6; March 31; May 1, 8, 19, 29; Aug 15; Oct 26; Nov 1; Dec 8, 24, 25, 26

Austrian Schilling travellers cheques not available in the UK but sterling cheques are widely accepted. Commission can be between ½ to 1½%. There is often a high minimum charge, say S30/40. So it's definitely not worth changing small amounts. The Uniform Eurocheque system is well developed and accepted in most places. Credit cards are also widely accepted. A very popular winter sports country for Britons and if you are going skiing make sure you have a good travel insurance policy with high medical cover limits – at least £500,000.

Belgium

Currency: Belgian Franc   100 centimes = 1 Belgian franc
Exchange Rate: £1 = 68.90 Belgian francs
Currency Restrictions: none

Banking Hours: 9–3.30pm, small branches close for lunch 1.00–2.30pm. Generally closed on Saturday except in tourist areas

National Holidays: Jan 1; March 31; May 19; July 11, 21; Aug 15; Nov 1, 11; Dec 25

Belgium Franc travellers cheques are not available in this country. Sterling cheques are acceptable but can be expensive to cash. This is because of the minimum commission per transaction of around B. Fr 100 (approx. £1.40). So make sure you don't cash small amounts of cheques. Credit cards are widely used, although you may have problems finding a bank which does Access or Visa cash withdrawals. The Uniform Eurocheque scheme is popular, particularly amongst traders. It is also the best alternative to getting cash from a bank.

Canada

Currency: Canadian Dollar   100 cents = Can $1

Exchange Rate: £1 = 1.984 Canadian dollars

Currency Restrictions: none

Banking Hours: 10.00–3.00pm Mon–Thurs, 10.00–6.00pm Fri, limited Saturday opening 10.00–3.00pm

National Holidays: Jan 1; March 28, 31; May 19; July 1; Sep 1; Oct 13; Nov 11; Dec 25, 26

Canadian dollar travellers cheques are widely available in this country. The golden rule for North America is to take only dollars, never sterling. You will find you can exist happily on a mix of Canadian dollar travellers cheques, credit and charge cards. If you are going across the border to the USA, take US dollar travellers cheques as Canadian ones can be difficult to cash. Travellers cheques are used as cash in both countries. The US dollar is widely accepted in Canada, but the exchange rate is different. Credit and charge cards are very useful. Make sure your limits are high enough before you leave the UK. All car hire companies will want a credit card with a voucher signed in blank.

Cyprus (Greek side)

Currency: Cyprus Pound   1000 Mils = Cyprus £1

Exchange Rate: £1 = 0.7680 Cyprus Pounds

Currency Restrictions: £50 Cyprus Pounds limit in and out

Banking Hours: 8.30–12.00 (Mon–Sat). Banks in some tourist areas open in mid-afternoon for foreign exchange transactions

National Holidays: Jan 1, 6; March 10, 25; May 1, 2, 3, 5; Aug 15; Oct 1, 28, 29; Dec 25, 26

Since the Turkish occupation of the Northern part, the main tourist areas are now concentrated in the Greek speaking south. Sterling travellers cheques are still the safest bet, although the Uniform Eurocheque scheme has been gaining in popularity. It is now widely accepted by local banks and can be used to withdraw cash. Credit cards are accepted in most hotels, restaurants and larger shops.

Denmark

Currency: Krone   100 Ore = 1 Danish krone

Exchange Rate: £1 = 12.2450 Danish krone

Currency Restrictions: only 5000 DKR can be exported unless more have been declared on entry

Banking Hours: 9.30–4.00pm in Copenhagen (Mon, Tues, Wed & Fri), 9.30–6.00pm on Thursday, in small towns late opening is on Friday rather than Thursday. Closed on Saturday

National Holidays: Jan 1; March 27, 28, 31; April 25; May 8, 19; June 5; Dec 25, 26

Danish krone travellers cheques are not available here, but sterling ones are acceptable. Normally there is a high minimum commission of approximately 20 KR (£1.60) so it's not worth cashing small amounts. The Uniform Eurocheque system is popular, particularly in tourist areas. Credit and charge cards are widely accepted.

France

Currency: French Franc   100 centimes = 1 FF

Exchange Rate: £1 = 10.20 French francs

Currency Restrictions: Normally exports limited to FF5,000 (approx. £460)

Banking Hours: Paris usually 9.00–4.30pm (Mon–Fri) and closed Saturday. Some banks close for lunch. Provinces also 9.00–4.30pm but some closed on Monday and open on Saturday

National Holidays: Jan 1; March 31; May 1, 8, 19; July 14; Aug 15; Nov 1, 11; Dec 25

The many banking networks in France often give rise to a wide range of exchange rates. So it is best to take French franc travellers cheques, which you should be able to cash without paying any extra commission. Sterling cheques are also acceptable, with a commission of about 10FF per transaction. The Uniform Euro-cheque system is popular throughout the country. However, because of the rivalry between the various banking groups, you may find you are directed to another bank on occasions because your cheques do not belong to a particular banking network. Credit and charge cards are widely accepted. Visa (sometimes called Carte Bleue) has many more outlets than Access/Mastercard.

Germany

Currency: Deutschmark   100 pfennigs = 1 Deutschmark

Exchange Rate: £1 = 3.3225 Deutschmarks

Currency Restrictions: None

Banking Hours: 9.00–1.00pm and 2.30–4.00pm (Mon–Fri) late opening Thursday, closed on Saturdays

National Holidays: Jan 1; March 28, 31; May 1, 8, 19; June 17; Nov 19; Dec 25, 26

German mark travellers cheques are available in the UK. However, sterling ones are equally useful and commissions range between ½ and 1½%.

The Uniform Eurocheque system is one of the most highly developed on the continent and is accepted just about everywhere. However, you cannot say the same about credit and charge cards. They are certainly used, but not with such wide popularity as in the UK for example. Not many garages will accept payment by plastic. Post offices open long hours and are a useful alternative for currency exchanges.

Greece

Currency: Drachma   100 lepta = 1 drachma

Exchange Rate: £1 = 204.16 drachma

Currency Restrictions: You can only take in or bring out a maximum of 3000 drachmas (approx. £15). Notes of more than 500 drachma should not be taken in or out

Banking Hours: 8.00–2.00pm (Mon–Fri). Closed Saturdays

National Holidays: Jan 1, 6; March 17, 25; May 1, 2, 5; June 23; Aug 15; Oct 28; Dec 25, 26

Drachma travellers cheques are not sold in this country. However sterling cheques are very suitable and generally speaking the rates offered are better than in the UK. You will be able to cash them in a wide variety of places – tourist offices, shops, hotels, restaurants, etc. The rate you get at banks will almost certainly be the most competitive, but beware of long queues and slow service. Bank commission is normally very low about 40 drachmas (20p) per £100 so you can cash small amounts without great expense.

You can also use Uniform Eurocheques to get cash out of a bank. Credit cards are widely accepted in the main tourist areas, but you won't be able to use them very much once you wander off the beaten track. Remember that Greece has many remote areas – islands – which will not have the same financial sophistication as the more popular parts. Always, have cash available when you are going off the beaten track.

Make sure you get rid of large currency notes before leaving the country – it is not only illegal to bring them out of the country, but you will also get a penal rate of exchange if you ask a UK bank to convert them back to sterling.

Holland

Currency: Guilders (also called Florins)   100 cents = 1 florin
Exchange Rate: £1 = 3.7525 guilders
Currency Restrictions: none
Banking Hours: 9.00–4.00p, (Mon–Fri). Closed on Saturdays
National Holidays: Jan 1; March 28, 31; May 8, 19; Dec 25, 26

Guilder travellers cheques available from Thomas Cook. However, you will have no problem with sterling ones. Minimum commission can be high (say 4 guilders) so do not cash small amounts.

Uniform Eurocheques are widely accepted and credit and charge cards also have plenty of outlets although you may find cash withdrawals difficult because of the limited number of banks which operate this facility.

Ireland

Currency: Punt   100 pence = 1 punt
Exchange Rate: £1 = 1.0982 punts
Restrictions: You cannot take out more than IR£100
Banking Hours: 10.00pm–12.30pm, 1.30–3.00pm; many banks are open until 5.00pm either Monday or Thursday. Most large banks are closed on Saturdays.
National Holidays: Jan 1; March 17, 31; June 2; Aug 4; Oct 27; Dec 25, 26

Irish punt travellers cheques are not available, but in any case, sterling ones are the best bet. Sterling cash is readily acceptable as well. Uniform Eurocheques and credit and charge cards are also popular, except in the remote country areas. Tourist offices are open long hours and will cash travellers cheques.

Italy

Currency: Lira
Exchange Rate: £1 = 2,260.75 lira
Currency Restrictions: No more than 400,000 can be taken in or out. You also cannot take out 100,000 notes

Banking Hours: 8.30–1.30pm and 3.00–4.00pm Mon–Fri. Closed Saturdays and in the afternoon on certain patron saints' days

National Holidays: Jan 1; March 31; April 25; May 1; Aug 15; Nov 1; Dec 8, 25, 26

You can buy Italian lira travellers cheques in this country, but they are not issued by the major companies. They will be drawn on local Italian banks and for this reason, you should stick to sterling ones. Italy has complex exchange controls and there may be refund problems if the cheques are lost or stolen. Commission on sterling cheques varies a great deal but there is normally a fixed minimum amount of about 1500 Lira (say 65p) which can make small encashments expensive. Be prepared for long queues in the banks. When they are closed, you can use tourist offices and travel bureaux which stay open late and give reasonable rates.

You are not allowed to export 100,000 lira notes so make sure you use them before you leave. If you take out 50,000 lira notes, expect a poor rate of exchange for them in the UK banks.

The Uniform Eurocheque system is popular in the tourist areas and most banks will cash them. Credit and charge cards are useful in the larger towns and tourist centres, although you may find cash withdrawals a problem. In addition many Italian garages will not take credit cards. In country areas it is best to rely on cash.

Luxembourg

Currency: Luxembourg Franc
             100 centimes = 1 Luxembourg franc
Exchange Rate: £1 = 68.00 Luxembourg francs
Currency Restrictions: None
Banking Hours: 8.30pm–12.00 noon; 1.30–4.30pm Mon–Fri. Closed Saturdays
National Holidays: Jan 1; March 31; May 1, 8, 19; June 23; Aug 15; Nov 1; Dec 25, 26

The Luxembourg franc is on the same exchange rate as the Belgian franc. Belgian currency is freely acceptable in Luxembourg (but not vice versa).

A small country with a highly sophisticated banking network. Sterling travellers cheques are acceptable but avoid cashing small amounts. The Uniform Eurocheque system is very well developed. All major charge and credit cards are widely accepted.

Malta

Currency: Maltese Pound   100 cents = 1 Maltese pound

Exchange Rate: £1 = 0.5780 Maltese pounds

Currency Restrictions: You take up to M£50 in and up to M£25 out

Banking Hours: 8.00–12.00 noon (Mon–Thurs), 8.00–12.00 noon, 1.30–4.00pm Friday, 8.00–11.30am Saturday. These are normal for summer months and there are winter variations

National Holidays: Jan 1; March 28, 31; May 1; Aug 15; Dec 13, 25

Sterling travellers cheques are acceptable but commission is high. It is normally charged on each cheque, around 12 cents per item (25p). So do not take lots of small denomination travellers cheques but go for bigger cheques.

British currency is widely accepted and many shops quote prices in sterling. Credit and charge cards are popular. The Uniform Eurocheque is accepted at all the bank, although they may be less widely accepted at shops, hotels and restaurants.

Morocco

Currency: Dirham   100 cents = 1 Dirham

Exchange Rate: £1 = 13.15 Dirham

Currency Restrictions: No import or export of Dirham allowed

Banking Hours: 8.15–11.30am and 2.15–4.00pm (Mon–Fri morning), 3.00–5.00pm Friday. Banks are closed on Saturdays. During Ramadan (approx. May 8–June 9) 9.30–3.30pm

National Holidays: Jan 1; March 3; May 1, 23; June 8, 9 ; July 9; Aug 14, 16, 17; Sep 6; Nov 6, 15, 16, 18

As you cannot take in the local currency, all money changing has to be done in Morocco. Sterling travellers cheques are best. Take some small denominations so you can cash only enough for your immediate needs. Spend your dirham before you go as you will have problems changing them back into pounds. In the past Uniform Eurocheques could only be used to cash at the bank and not all banks belong to the scheme. However, the retail sector has now been allowed to join this system, so you will find an increasing number of shops will take them. Credit cards are accepted in the popular tourist areas, but cash is still the best bet. Remember that bargaining for goods is a way of life in Morocco – and cash is essential if you are going to get a good deal.

Norway

Currency: Krone   100 Ore = 1 Norwegian krone
Exchange Rate: £1 = 10.3550 Norwegian krone
Currency Restrictions: You can't take out more than 5000 krone
Banking Hours: 8.15–3.00pm Mon–Fri late opening Thursday. Closed Saturdays
National Holidays: Jan 1; March 26, 27, 28, 31; May 1, 8, 17, 19; Dec 24, 25, 26, 31

Krone travellers cheques are unavailable here but sterling ones are quite satisfactory. However, watch out for high commission charges – often 6 krone (60p) per cheque. This makes small cheques expensive to cash

The Uniform Eurocheques are well established and accepted in most areas. Credit cards are popular in large cities but not widely used in the country, and not many garages seem to take them.

Portugal

Currency: Escudo   100 centavos = 1 escudo
Exchange Rate: £1 = 217.0 escudos
Currency Restrictions: No more than 5000 in or out of the country
Banking Hours: 8.30–11.45am, 1pm–2.45pm, Mon–Fri. Closed Saturdays.

National Holidays: Jan 1; Feb 11; March 27, 28; Apr 25; May 1, 29; June 10, 13, 24; July 1; Aug 15, 21; Oct 5; Nov 1; Dec 1, 8, 24, 25, 26

Although escudo travellers cheques are available in the UK, sterling cheques are widely accepted. Be wary of taking escudo travellers cheques issued by local banks as you may have problems with the refund service. Commission is low on travellers cheques, and some banks don't charge at all. The rates of exchange given are normally better in Portugal than they are in the UK. Tourist offices open long hours and will cash travellers cheques.

The Uniform Eurocheque system is well developed in the tourist areas but not elsewhere. Credit and charge cards are much the same, plenty of outlets in the popular resorts but not off the beaten track. Not many garages accept plastic cards.

Spain

Currency: Peseta   100 cents = 1 peseta
Exchange Rate: £1 = 209.30 pesetas
Currency Restrictions: Unlimited amounts in, 100,000 (approx. £450) out
Banking Hours: 9.00–2.00pm (Mon–Fri), 9.00–1.00pm Sat
National Holidays: Jan 1, 6, 22; March 19, 27, 28, 29, 31; May 1, 2, 15, 19, 29; July 15, 31; Aug 15; Oct 12; Nov 1; Dec 8, 25, 26

Now a fully fledged member of the Common Market, Spain has been in the holiday business for a long time. Sterling travellers cheques are the best bet, and you normally get a better exchange rate in Spain than you do in the UK. Commission is about 1% though it can be higher.

Uniform Eurocheques are widely accepted. If you are a customer of the Midland or National Westminster you can use the Eurocheque card to get money out of cash machines in certain areas. Credit and plastic cards are very popular. VISA can also be used for cash withdrawals at banks in many areas. Travel agents are open long hours and cash most forms of money.

Sweden

Currency: Krona   100 ore = 1 Swedish krona

Exchange Rate: £1 = 10.5225 krona

Currency Restrictions: Limited to 6,000 in or out

Banking Hours: 9.30–3.00pm Mon–Fri also many banks open from 4.00 or 4.30 to 5.30–6.00pm. Closed on Saturdays

National Holidays: Jan 1, 6; March 28, 31; May 1, 8, 19; June 20, 21; Nov 1; Dec 24, 25, 26, 31

Swedish krona travellers cheques are not available here, but sterling ones are perfectly acceptable. Minimum commission can be high – perhaps 15 krona (£1.45) so it is very expensive to cash small amounts. Uniform Eurocheques are well developed and credit and charge cards are widely accepted.

Switzerland

Currency: Swiss Franc   100 cents = 1 Swiss franc

Exchange Rate: £1 = 2.7350 Swiss francs

Currency Restrictions: none

Banking Hours: 8.30–4.30 Mon–Fri. Closed Saturdays

National Holidays: Jan 1, 2; March 28, 31; May 8, 19; Dec 25, 26. There are wide variations in the different Cantons

A highly sophisticated financial centre with many banks even in small towns. Both sterling and Swiss franc travellers cheques are acceptable and generally most banks do not charge commission. The Unform Eurocheque system is widely accepted and so too are all the major credit and charge cards. But not many banks will advance cash against VISA or Access.

Some Swiss towns, particularly in skiing resorts, have declared themselves 'cashless' and you can rely on plastic to pay for everything – even Doctor's bills and clinics if you are unfortunate enough to suffer an accident on a skiing holiday.

Tunisia

Currency: Dinar   1000 mils = 1 dinar

Exchange Rate: £1 = 1,0200 dinars

Currency Restrictions: No import or export of Dinars allowed

Banking Hours: 8–11.00am, 2.00–4.15pm Mon–Fri. May 20–June 20 8.00–2.00pm, June 21–Sept 15 7.00–1.00pm. Closed on Saturdays

National Holidays: Jan 1; March 20; April 9; May 1; June 1, 3, 9; July 25; Aug 3, 13, 15; Sep 3, 6; Oct 15; Nov 15

Take sterling travellers cheques, which can be cashed at banks and hotels free of charge. Exchange rates are the same everywhere. Take some small denomination cheques to cover your short term needs. Don't forget you can't take any dinar with you out of the country, so make sure you spend them all before your departure. Eurocheques can be used only to get money out of banks. Credit and charge cards are accepted in the tourist areas.

Turkey

Currency: Lire   100 kurus = 1 lire

Exchange Rate: £1 = 839.10 lire

Currency Restrictions: None going in, 300,000 (approx. £370) can be taken out

Banking Hours: 8.30–12.00 noon, 1.30–5.00pm Mon–Fri. Closed on Saturdays – local variations in tourist areas

National Holidays: Jan 1; April 23; May 19; June 9, 10, 11; Aug 15, 16, 17, 18, 19, 30; Oct 19

Although there are no restrictions on bringing in lire, it's not really worth it. The Turkish tourist board say that the exchange rates in Turkey are usually much better than you will get in the UK. One traveller reported last year that the exchange rate in Turkey was 20% more favourable than the UK rate. Take sterling travellers cheques – commission rates are normally very low.

You can use Uniform Eurocheques at most banks, but not in the retail sector. Credit and charge cards are accepted in larger cities and tourist areas, but you will not be able to use them in remote areas.

USA

Currency: Dollar   100 cents = 1 US dollar
Exchange Rate: £1 = 1.205 US dollars
Currency Restrictions: none
Banking Hours: 9.00–3.00pm Mon–Fri, closed Saturdays. There are variations in the different States, some late night opening. There are over 14,000 different banks
National Holidays: Jan 1, 20; Feb 17; May 26; July 4; Sept 1; Oct 13; Nov 11, 27; Dec 25

The USA is much closer to becoming a cashless society than any other country. You will find that a mixture of dollar travellers cheques, charge and credit cards will do very nicely. Travellers cheques are used in the same way as cash. Banks normally do not charge a commission to exchange them. Don't take sterling travellers cheques as these are often difficult to cash.

All credit and charge cards are accepted and in fact are essential for car hire. Make sure your limits are high enough before you leave home.

Yugoslavia

Currency: New Dinar   100 paras = 1 new dinar
Exchange Rate: £1 = 446.71 new dinars
Currency Restrictions: 2500 dinar (approx £6) in or out
Banking Hours: 7.00–7.00pm Mon–Fri, 8.00–1.00pm Saturdays
National Holidays: Jan 1, 2; May 1, 2; July 4; Nov 29, 30; Dec 1. There are other regional holidays

Take sterling travellers cheques. They can be cashed at banks, hotels, tourist offices and post offices anywhere in the country. The rate is the same everywhere, and there is no commission. Keep some small denomination travellers cheques for immediate needs. You cannot change back unused dinars and can only take out 2500.

If you are driving you will need petrol coupons. You can only buy them with foreign currency at the border, or in banks and tourist agencies. You can also buy dinar cheques with foreign currency at banks, post offices and tourist agencies. These are not travellers cheques, but discount vouchers and are treated as cash. But if you lose them they are not replaceable. They give you 10% discount at restaurants, hotels, tours, etc. Not all privately owned restaurants belong to the scheme. They can take a long time to process both when buying and selling. But you can change them back to pounds if you still have the purchase slip. The Uniform Eurocheque scheme can be used at banks to get cash and at a few retail outlets. Plastic cards are accepted in the main tourist areas.

Note: Currency rates as at 17 February 1986 throughout

GUIDE TO BANKNOTE REGULATIONS

"Known in the business as FOLDING MONEY"

Country	Currency unit	You may take in	You may bring out
Afghanistan	Afghani	Unlimited	1000
Albania	Lek	None	None
Algeria	Alg. Dinar	None	None
Andorra	Fr. Franc/Sp. Peseta	As for France/Spain	
Angola	Kwanza	None	None
Argentina	Austral	Unlimited	Unlimited
Australia	Aus. Dollar	Unlimited	5000
Austria	Schilling	Unlimited	15000
Bahamas	Bah. Dollar	70	70
Bahrain	Bah. Dinar	Unlimited	Unlimited
Bangladesh	Taka	100	100
Barbados	Barb. Dollar	Unlimited	100
Belgium	Bel. Franc	Unlimited	Unlimited
Belize	Bel. Dollar	100	100
Benin	C.F.A. Franc	Unlimited	25000
Bermuda	Berm. Dollar	Unlimited	250
Bhutan	Ind. Rupee	None	None
Bolivia	Bol. Peso	Unlimited	Unlimited
Botswana	Pula	Unlimited	75
Brazil	Curzeiro	Unlimited	Unlimited
Brunei	Brun. Dollar	Unlimited	Unlimited
Bulgaria	Lev	None	None
Burma	Kyat	None	None
Burundi	Bur. Franc	2·000	2·000
Cameroon	C.F.A. Franc	Unlimited	50000
Canada	Can. Dollar	Unlimited	Unlimited
Cape Verde Is.	C.V. Escudo	None	None
Caymen Is.	C. I. Dollar	Unlimited	Unlimited
Central Afr. Rep.	C.F.A. Franc	Unlimited	50000
Chad	C.F.A. Franc	Unlimited	10000
Chile	New Chil. Peso	Unlimited	Unlimited
China	Renminbi	None	None
Colombia	Col. Peso	500	500
Comoro Is.	C.F.A. Franc	Unlimited	50000
Congo	C.F.A. Franc	Unlimited	50000
Costa Rica	Colon	Unlimited	Unlimited
Cuba	Cuban Peso	None	None
Cyprus	Cyp. Pound	50	50
Czechoslovakia	Koruna	None	None
Denmark	Dan. Krone	Unlimited	50000
Djibouti	Dji. Franc	Unlimited	Unlimited
Dominican Rep.	Dom. Peso	None	None
*East Caribbean	E.C. Dollar	Unlimited	Unlimited
Ecuador	Sucre	Unlimited	Unlimited
Egypt	Egypt. Pound	20	20

Country	Currency unit	You May take in	You May bring out
El Salvador	Colon	200	200
Equatorial Guinea	Ekuele	None	None
Ethiopia	Eth. Birr	None	None
Falkland Isl.	F.I. Pound	Unlimited	Unlimited
Faroe Is.	Danish Krone	Unlimited	50000
Fiji	Fiji. Dollar	Unlimited	Unlimited
Finland	Markka	Unlimited	10000
France	Franc	Unlimited	5000
French Guiana	Fr. Franc	Unlimited	5000
French Pacific	C.F.P. Franc	Unlimited	90000
French West Indies	Fr. Franc	Unlimited	5000
Gabon	C.F.A. Franc	Unlimited	25000
Gambia	Dalasi	Unlimited	75
Germany DR	Ost Mark	None	None
Germany W	Deutsche Mark	Unlimited	Unlimited
Ghana	Cedi	None	None
Gibraltar	Gib. Pound	Unlimited	Unlimited
Greece	Drachma (Notes 500 and smaller)	3000	3000
Greenland	Dan. Krone	Unlimited	50000
Guatamala	Quetzal	Unlimited	Unlimited
Guinea	Syli	None	None
Guinea Bissau	G.B. Esc	None	None
Guyana	Guy. Dollar	40	40
Haiti	Gourde	Unlimited	Unlimited
Honduras	Lempira	Unlimited	Unlimited
Hong Kong	H.K. Dollar	Unlimited	Unlimited
Hungary	Forint (100 in coin in and out)	None	None
Iceland	I. Krona	8000	8000
India	Ind. Rupee	None	None
Indonesia	Rupiah	50000	50000
Iran	Ir. Rial	20000	20000
Iraq	Ir. Dinar	25	5
Irish Rep.	Irish Pound (Notes 20 and smaller)	Unlimited	100
Israel	Is. Shekel	Unlimited	500
Italy	Lira	400000	400000
Ivory Coast	C.F.A. Franc	Unlimited	25000
Jamaica	Jam. Dollar	None	None
Japan	Yen	Unlimited	3000.000
Jordan	Jor. Dinar	Unlimited	300
Kampuchea	Riel	None	None
Kenya	K. Shilling	None	None
Kiribati	Aust. Dollar	Unlimited	250

123

Country	Currency unit	You may take in	You may bring out
Korea (North)	Won	None	None
Korea (South)	Won	500000	500000
Kuwait	Kuw. Dinar	Unlimited	Unlimited
Laos	Kip	None	None
Lebanon	Leb. Pound	Unlimited	Unlimited
Lesotho	Maloti	100	100
Liberia	Lib. Dollar	Unlimited	Unlimited
Libya	Libyan Dinar	None	None
Liechtenstein	Swiss Franc	Unlimited	Unlimited
Luxembourg	Lux. Franc	Unlimited	Unlimited
Macao	Pataca	Unlimited	Unlimited
Malagasy Rep.	Mal. Franc	5000	5000
Malawi	Kwacha	20	20
Malaysia	Ringgit	Unlimited	Unlimited
Maldive Is.	Rufiyaa	Unlimited	Unlimited
Mali	Mali. Franc	Unlimited	50000
Malta	Mal. Pound	50	25
Mauritania	Ouguiya	None	None
Mauritius	Mau. Rupee	700	350
Mexico	Mex. Peso	Unlimited	Unlimited
Monaco	Fr. Franc	Unlimited	5000
Mongolia	Tugrik	None	None
Morocco	Mor. Dirham	None	None
Mozambique	Metica	None	None
Namibia	S.A. Rand	200	200
Nauru	Aust. Dollar	Unlimited	5000
Nepal	Nep. Rupee	None	None
Netherlands	Guilder	Unlimited	Unlimited
Neth. Antilles	Neth. Ant. Guilder	200	200
New Zealand	N.Z. Dollar	Unlimited	Unlimited
Nicaragua	Cordoba	Unlimited	Unlimited
Niger	C.F.A. Franc	Unlimited	25000
Nigeria	Naira	20	20
Norway	Nor.Krone	Unlimited	2000
Oman	Om. Rial	Unlimited	Unlimited
Pakistan	Pak. Rupee	100	100
Panama	Balboa	Unlimited	Unlimited
Papua N.G.	Kina	Unlimited	200
Paraguay	Guarani	Unlimited	Unlimited
Peru	Inti	Unlimited	Unlimited
Phillipines	Phil. Peso	500	500
Poland	Zloty	None	None
Portugal	Port. Escudo	10000	10000
Puerto Rico	U.S. Dollar	Unlimited	Unlimited
Qatár	Q. Riyal	Unlimited	Unlimited

Country	Currency unit	You may take in	You may bring out
Reunion	Fr. Franc	Unlimited	5000
Romania	Leu	None	None
Rwanda	Rw. Franc	5000	5000
St. Helena	St. H. Pound	Unlimited	Unlimited
St. Pierre and Miquelon	Fr. Franc	Unlimited	5000
Sao Tome et Ppe	Dobra	None	None
Saudi Arabia	Saudi Riyal	Unlimited	Unlimited
Senegal	C.F.A. Franc	Unlimited	25000
Seychelles	S. Rupee	Unlimited	Unlimited
Sierra Leone	Leone	20	20
Singapore	Sing. Dollar	Unlimited	Unlimited
Solomon Is.	S.I. Dollar	Unlimited	250
Somali Rep.	Som. Shilling	200	200
South Africa	S.A. Rand	200	200
Spain	Pesetas	Unlimited	100000
Sri Lanka	S.L. Rupee	250	250
Sudan	Sud. Pound	None	None
Surinam	S. Guilder	100	100
Swaziland	Lilangeni	100	100
Sweden	S. Krona	Unlimited (Notes 1000 & smaller)	6000
Switzerland	Swiss Franc	Unlimited	Unlimited
Syria	Sy. Pound	100	100
Taiwan	New Taiwan Dollar	8000	8000
Tanzania	Tan. Shilling	None	None
Thailand	Baht	2000	500
Togo	C.F.A. Franc	Unlimited	50000
Tonga	Pa'anga	Unlimited	50
Trinidad & Tobago	T. & T. Dollar (Notes 20 and smaller)	200	200
Tunisia	Tun. Dinar	None	None
Turkey	Tur. Liras	Unlimited	Equiv. U.S.$ 1000
Tuvalu	Aust. Dollar	Unlimited	5000
Uganda	Ug. Shilling	None	None
Un. Arab Emirates	U.A.E. Dirham	Unlimited	Unlimited
United Kingdom	Sterling Pound	Unlimited	Unlimited
USA	U.S. Dollar	Unlimited	Unlimited
Upper Volta	C.F.A. Franc	Unlimited	25000
Uruquay	Ur. Peso	Unlimited	Unlimited
U.S.S.R.	Rouble	None	None
Vanuatu	Vatu	Unlimited	Unlimited
Vatican	It. Lire	200.000 (Notes 50000 and smaller)	200.000
Venezuela	Bolivia	Unlimited	Unlimited
Vietnam	Dong	None	None

Country	Currency unit	You may take in	You may bring out
Virgin Is.	U.S. Dollar	Unlimited	Unlimited
Western Samoa	Tala	None	None
Yemen (North)	Riyal	Unlimited	Unlimited
Yemen (South)	Y. Dinar	5	5
Yugoslavia	Yug. Dinar	5000	5000
	(Once a year. Subsequently 2000 in and out during the same ye		
	(Notes 1000 and smaller)		
Zaire	Zaire	None	None
Zambia	Zam. Kwacha	10	10
Zimbabwe	Zim. Dollar	20	20

*EAST CARIBBEAN: Antigua, Dominica, Grenada, Monserrat, St. Kitts-Nevis, Anguilla, St. Lucia, St. Vincent

§ FRENCH PACIFIC: New Caledonia, French Polynesia, Wallis and Futuna

† FRENCH WEST INDIES: Guadeloupe & Dependencies, Martinique

‡ UNITED ARAB EMIRATES: Abu Dhabi, Ajman, Dubai, Fujairah, Ras-Al-Khahmah, Sharjah, Umm-Al-Qawain

Source: Thomas Cook

Please note, regulations change frequently. So double check before your departure.

Rosemary Burr's Money Book

A useful aid to sound budgeting. It includes twelve monthly expenditure record sheets plus a dozen helpful hints on money matters.

'If you've ever wondered where your money goes. Rosemary Burr's Money Book should supply you with the answers and help you keep a regular track on your spending and saving. The book comprises an easy check-list for expenses with useful tips on all financial aspects.' *Woman's Realm*

'Writing down every single item is the best way to check on your spending. A cleverly designed paperback "Money Book" by financial expert Rosemary Burr might just inspire you to do it.' Katie Boyle, *TV Times*

Also recommended, *Sunday Telegraph*, *Observer*, *Ideal Home*, *Good Housekeeping* and *Personal Finance & Investment*.
Price: 87p

Funny Money by Alan Ralph

If you thought money was no laughing matter then this collection of cartoons by Alan Ralph, a regular contributor to The Guardian Weekend Money columns, should change your mind.

'His cartoons are sharp and often merciless . . . and frequently remind those who have control over our money that we can kick back. The cartoons rate more than a casual glance.' *The Guardian*

'If they don't make you chuckle perhaps your bank manager might see the funny side of things next time you call on him.' *The Times*

'If these witty one liners had you holding your sides then this could be the light reading for the train you've been looking for. Ralph has blown up a few myths about the institutions by breaking through the jargon and mystification.' *Money Marketing*

ISBN 0 948032 00 6   Price: £2.99